ALLY MCBEAL:
THE TOTALLY UNAUTHORIZED GUIDE

ALLY MCBEAL:
THE TOTALLY UNAUTHORIZED GUIDE

By Kathy Mitchell

WARNER BOOKS

A Time Warner Company

Thanks to J.D. Heiman, Abigail Howe Heiman, Katherine Howe, Billy and Emma Howe Heiman, Lynn Harris, Florence Harris, John Shaughnessey, Juliet Siler, Fawn Fitter, Drew Chase, the folks at DWAI and BPVP, Steven Jablonoski, Kieran Scott, Casey Greenfield, Adam Lehner and Dana Hagerty.

Warner Books, Inc.
1271 Avenue of the Americas
New York, NY 10020

Visit our Web site at http://warnerbooks.com

 A Time Warner Company

Printed in the United States of America

First Printing: October 1998

10 9 8 7 6 5 4 3 2 1

ISBN: 0-446-67532-6

LC: 98-86739

A GLC Book

Cover design by Ross George
Design by Ross George

Cover photo courtesy of EVERETT PHOTOS; © 20TH-CENTURY FOX
Back cover photo courtesy of OUTLINE; ©GEORGE LANGE

"Should this miniskirted neurotic be a role model?"

—London's *Daily Mail*

McBeal Appeal

Irresistible television, whether you experience it as a sexual differences safari or as a blueprint for your own life. —*Ken Tucker,* Entertainment Weekly

Not so long ago, television at the beginning of the workweek was a deadly dull affair, dominated by Aaron Spelling's sponsored schlock and that musty, tube-sock-wearing juggernaut known as *Monday Night Football*. If you didn't happen to think Wisconsin cheddar made for chic headgear or that a pair of teased hussies trying to drown each other in a Jacuzzi was synonymous with the phrase "that's entertainment," you were practically compelled to curl up with a good book.

Until Ally came along.

Let's take a moment. A year ago most of us would have thought a Fishism related to muskellunge or Abe Vigoda. Poughkeepsie was just a town in New York. Bygones were, well, bygones.

Then *Ally McBeal* shimmied into the Monday evening lineup, sorting through a Filene's Basement bag full of post-feminist neuroses to Vonda Shepard piano-bar tunes. In a single season a leggy Beantown attorney with Walter Mitty-esque daydreams and a train wreck for a love life has become our end-of-the-millennium It-Girl. And quirky McBealisms invaded the lexicon faster than flesh-eating bacteria colonized the Congo.

She is a sensation, but Ally's success—especially on a network previously associated with such thinking-women's fare as *America's Scariest Police Chases*—was anything close to a foregone conclusion. True, when *Ally McBeal* slipped into the slot behind *Melrose Place* in September 1997, it garnered the highest ratings of any Fox show in the time slot since 1989, but the initial competition was mostly reruns. Later in its maiden season the show was not only

GLOBE PHOTOS

crushed under the cleats of the great gridiron Goliath, it often trailed the dried-up football widows who made up NBC's anemic "Must She TV." Fox programmers also did their part to help Ally get lost on the fall schedule, pre-empting the show a few times to make way for gems like *When Animals Attack*.

Luckily Ally worked a little magic on her own, surviving those wobbly first few weeks to morph into nothing less than a pop-culture phenomenatrix. How did an Ivy League-educated misfit with a briefcase filled with hangups get voted Ms. Zeitgeist, 1998? What did Ally have that Susan, Caroline, Cybill, or Kirstie Alley squeezed into a feathery negligee lacked? Well, plenty of Ooga-chaka, for starters. Plus quirky stuff such as unisex bathrooms;

a grown man nicknamed after a baked good; assorted wattle, tooth and cross-dressing fetishes; group marriages; smile therapy; face bras; dancing babies; dancing twins; and even dancing lawyers. While other TV comedy divas were surrounded by mix-and-match casts of Gap ad rejects, Ally's wacked-out colleagues, from reptilian WASP Richard Fish to nutty, slutty and proud-of-it Elaine Vassal, were unforgettable. And besides sporting a killer wardrobe, Ally accessorized with some of the sharpest writing in the medium, courtesy of her creator David Kelley.

What truly made *Ally McBeal* a hit, though, was a little thing we'll call McBuzz. Even after repeated viewings, most people couldn't remember if the name of the girl who starred in *The Naked Truth* was Tanya, Theda or Tia Maria. But even a brief visit to that co-ed commode got people talking. Not talking so much as bickering, really. Loudly. Indeed, Ally managed to provoke more water-cooler arguments than any TV character since Murphy Brown, who sent Vice President Dan Quayle scurrying to his speechwriter.

Thus the Great Ally Debate began. Kickboxing in one corner were those

> *"The one thing I don't buy about* Ally McBeal's *breakout success is that people are watching it because Ally herself is a postfeminist role model.* Ally McBeal, *stripped to its essentials, is a program about a young woman with an interesting job who can't quite get her life together. Yet* The Naked Truth, Suddenly Susan, *and* Caroline in the City *all focus on beautiful, talented young women who can't quite get their lives together. And nobody's talking about them."*
>
> —*Joe Queenan,* TV Guide

convinced that the dizzy, dishy Gen X lawyer was more than just a hoot: she spoke the sad, funny truths of young single women's lives. In the other corner were the equally passionate Against Ally's, who found the series little more than a cutesy update of a *Cathy* cartoon starring a whiny, pre-feminism throwback who was, by the way, way too damned skinny. And sitting in the audience watching the ref run back and forth were those of us who just thought *Ally McBeal* was good escapist fun.

ners, or just cloying and never that clever? Was singer Vonda Shepard TV's melodious answer to Joni Mitchell or a grating Lilith Fair Barbie doll? McBuzz crackled all year long, devouring column inches in heavy hitters such as the *Newsweek*, the *L.A. Times*, and *The Washington Post*, as well as ricocheting endlessly through cyberspace.

Unfortunately for Ally-bashers, the heated chatter lured an audience better than the work of a thousand network-jingle writers. Buoyed by McBuzz, *Ally*

"Herman's Head *meets* My So-Called Life *meets* Dream On *meets* Molly Dodd *meets* Nine-to-Five *meets . . . you get the idea.*"

—*Lynne Harris*, New York Daily News

Entertainment Weekly hailed Ally as "irresistible," while the *Village Voice* found her "loathsome." Beltway pundit Maureen Dowd thought Ally's unrepentant girly-girlishness signaled a healthy feminization of the workplace, but over at *The New Republic*, Lexis-Nexis-challenged scribe Ruth Shalit saw only retro ditzy-ness dressed up as Grrl Power. And it wasn't only Ally that elicited strong reactions, but nearly every aspect of her glossy, *My-So-Called-Nine-To-Five* life. Was the show a clever comedy of contemporary man-

McBeal now has more than 15 million viewers. Our pint-sized, prat-falling barrister not only whupped the Prada pants off the Peacock Network competition, but drove a stake clear through the WB's *Buffy the Vampire Slayer*, who skulked off to wrassle the undead on Tuesday nights. The *Ally McBeal* sound track CD, filled with Vonda Shepard covers of daisy-decal goo like "Hooked on a Feeling" and "Walk Away Renee," has gone gold. In short, *Ally McBeal* is indubitably a runaway hit, snagging a pair of Golden Globe awards—one for best comedy series, and the other for actress Calista Flockhart, the woman who made Ally a star, and became a star herself in the process.

The jury is in. Love her, hate her—beg her to eat more than a single rice cake for dinner—there is no denying that Ally tripped over a major cultural chord in those chunky Kenneth Cole heels. Political pundits continue to decry her cotton-candy musings about life, love and litigation; feminist theorists can't stop scrapping over whether her Band-Aid–size skirts and unrepentant man hunger are, sigh, Good for Feminism. It won't be long before people start dubbing plucky young women McBeals.

But whether we think Ally is Superwoman or Loserwoman, why must she be a stand-in for Everywoman? It's high time to flush that notion down the Unisex crapper. After all, nobody critiques Frasier for being a poor role model for men or slams the *Friends* lads for sitting in a coffee shop while real twentysomething males watch the World Cup. See, guys, being guys, just get to be funny. Ally, on the other hand, is forced to work an extra shift to represent and uplift all females everywhere. Did somebody just order a half-caffe Double Standard?

This unfair situation breeds dismay all over the map. When Ally comes home from a date complaining about *not* being groped, alarm bells go off at women's studies departments and irate op-ed writers run for their laptops to plonk out screeds about whether such wishes threaten to send women back to the dreaded "I Feel Pretty" days. Do they? (And furthermore, what's wrong with feeling pretty?) It depends on whether you view feminism's glass as half-empty or half-full. If your perspective is the former, Ally's forays into *Cosmo* country are proof that she's a fem-bot launched by Phyllis Schlafly to bring America's female TV viewers back to the 1950s fold. But if your worldview is closer to the latter, then Ally's departures from doctrine indicate

> *"The new Mary Tyler Moore? Ally McBeal is more like the female Austin Powers, minus the irony; the show is a defrosted throwback to leering '70s 'liberated chick' series like* Charlie's Angels *and* Police Woman. *Except that writer/producer David Kelley is luring you in with an intellectual jiggle."*
>
> —*Joyce Millman*, Salon

just how far we've come, and just how far we can go.

Sure, Ally can be a whiner. But the beautiful part is that she is free to be one. She's a post–*Feminine Mystique* gal, secure enough in her liberation to whine about it. Sainted feminist icon Mary Richards—with whom Ally is frequently and unfairly compared—never dared to whine. Heck, Mare never called her boss by his first name, let alone boogied with a transvestite hooker. Ally's sex life may be far from perfect, but at least we know it exists (and that when it's on the wane, she's stockpiling tubes of contraceptive jelly for when things brighten up). Unlike Mary, Ally *knows* she can make it on her own; she just isn't sure she wants to. And what's more, as Calista Flockhart patiently pointed out to reporters over the show's tumultuous

first year, Ally McBeal is something rather new in a TV heroine, something Mary couldn't afford to be: a deliciously *lousy* role model. She can hardly get out of bed some mornings, let alone turn the whole world on with her smile (although tooth fetishist Judge Happy Boyle might disagree).

If Ally's whom we've elected our latest TV sweetheart, she's the one we deserve in these uncertain times. The 1950s loved Lucy's kid glove rebellion against Ricky-Knows-Best male authority. The 1960s went kooky for Ann Marie's go-go-booted tiptoe through the sexual revolution, and the 1970s will forever be known as the Mary decade. In the 1980s, we were introduced to Molly Dodd (whose hyperactive imagination would give Ally's a run for the Prozac), but that decade really belonged to Reaganette Alexis Carrington, who could teach those *Melrose Place* vixens a thing or two about shattering a glass of Cristal.

With the exception of Alexis, who was really just another pair of shoulder pads in a long line of deliciously bitchy actresses stretching back to Bette Davis, we wouldn't mind having any of these actresses in our carpools (jaunts to the Vitametavegamin factory

> "Ally McBeal is a slap in the face of the real-life working girl, a weekly insult to the woman who wants sexual freedom and gender equality, who can date and litigate in the same week without collapsing in a Vagisil heap."
>
> —Ruth Shalit, The New Republic

notwithstanding). That's because at bottom, all these actresses had more than a sense of humor in common. All were permanently, hopelessly, and irrevocably nice. One look at *Ally McBeal*'s distaff comedy competition shows how little times have changed. From Dharma to Caroline, under wafer-thin veneers of kookiness lie vast, sickly-sweet quantities of—you guessed it—the dreaded *N*-word.

Ally, on the other hand, is nicer on the outside, but inside she's a mess, and not always a nice one. As her theme-song-lovin' therapist Dr. Tracey Clark puts it, she is a "cracker" and a "weakling." Even her best friend, the rock-solid Renee Radick, is often convinced Ally's a wacko—at the very least. Renee's got a point. This is, after all, a Harvard-trained attorney who fears criminals, flirts compulsively with her married ex-boyfriend and avoids important meetings with clients because she can't help feeling like a

wittle girl. Worst of all, she has the temerity to voice such heresies as: "All I ever wanted to be was rich and successful and to have three kids and a husband waiting for me at night to tickle my feet. And look at me—I don't even like my hair!"

As *The New York Times* famously put it, "You want to smack Ally McBeal, but do you like her?" Not always. And in that ambiguity lies the secret of McBeal Appeal. No matter how much we identify with her career angst and thudding biological clock, we often can't decide if Ally's behavior makes her irresistible or loathsome (and come to think of it, that's a large part of Ally's problem, too).

Like so many of us in the audience, Ally's a backsliding mass of contradictions, a Soul Sister who regularly battles with her inner Stepford Wife and doesn't always win. When Georgia, an island of sanity in Ally's emotional whirlpool, demands to know why Ally thinks her problems are so much bigger than everybody else's, Ally answers: "Because they're mine." Nice girls think such thoughts, but they don't dare utter them. Ally's not only sprung herself from the stifling girdle of Niceness worn by Mary and all the rest of her comedy predecessors, sometimes she positively sounds like George Costanza in a minidress.

We love that in her conflicted heart, Ally truly is a nice girl who wants to do the right thing. But we also love that she's a nice girl who sometimes does the wrong, selfish, petty thing. By behaving badly, she's led us out of the era of Woman-as-Role-Model and into the golden age of Woman-as-Human-Being.

Not that this human being inhabits a world anywhere approximating a real one. It should be clear that any resemblance between Ally's occupation and that of a real corporate lawyer is purely coincidental. Allyland is a subversively trippy place, where coworkers form kick-lines to Burt Bacharach tunes and moon-lit evenings are an invitation to dance in the middle of the street in

sheep-print PJs. *Ally McBeal* is a television dramady that's gleefully unmoored itself from realism even as it allows its main character to fall on her delicate face. What a perfect romantic comedy for the 1990s—one in which the damsel prefers being distressed, the best friend isn't comic relief, and the Other Woman is more sympathetic than the heroine.

A word from the bench. Whatever you make of all the McBuzz, in the end you must commend Ally McBeal. She's forever raised the bar (and possibly, the hemlines) for TV heroines to come. And as for sitcom conventions? Well, bygones. Here's hoping Ally keeps tripping along, and making us laugh, as she searches her soul. Her flaws may forever bar her from becoming a crisply competent, eternally sanguine and thoroughly commendable role model. But they've made her something better: imminently, and irresistibly, watchable.

Ally-World

The most oft-voiced, enduring, and silliest knock made against *Ally McBeal* is that it isn't *realistic*.

The criticism goes something like this:

Never in a million flushes would a corporate law firm, especially one in uptight Boston, install a unisex bathroom. Furthermore, 28-year-old associates at such firms are swathed in starchy Brooks Brothers suits and Cole Haan shoes, not gadding about in sexy thigh-baring numbers. Genuine associates spend most of their days (and nights) getting eyestrain sifting through mountains of impossibly dry documents, not making like Clarence Darrow in one impossibly kooky, kinky jury trial after another—in fact, they are lucky to ever even see a courtroom outside of TV. Moreover, psychiatrists agree that picking a bubblegum oldie for a personal theme song is not a recommended cure for depression and that even the frothiest cappuccino is unlikely to approximate the pleasures of sexual foreplay.

Well, duh.

Hello, killjoys! This is a *television show*. *On Fox*. One that follows that hard-hitting workplace drama . . . *Melrose Place*. If *Ally McBeal* holds a mirror up to the working world, it's strictly of the fun-house variety.

Imagine, if you will, a show called *Real McBeal*. Each episode would open with Ally in dowdy dress-for-success wear, drinking her sixtieth black cup of Java in a dingy cubicle with unflattering overhead fluorescent lighting. Later on we'd see a zany run-in with ex-boyfriend William by the fax machine, in which the pair would share two minutes of uneasy banter about the last episode of *Seinfeld* before fleeing back to their cubbyholes. The plot would only get wackier as the hour went on—Ally's hyperefficient assistant, Elaine, could provide some belly laughs in the form of a Dilbert cartoon taped to her boss's computer terminal. Then we'd get to see our heroine drag home a box full of files to her austere apartment at midnight, soak her swollen feet in a mixing bowl filled with Epsom salts, and call her friend Renee (whom she hasn't seen in three months) to cancel weekend plans yet again. ("Sorry, Renee, but you know. Gotta work.") Around three o'clock in the morning, our Real McBeal would collapse in an exhausted heap on her couch next to a half-eaten carton of Ben & Jerry's, a dangerously uncapped highlighter, and her cat, Twinkle. Then the camera would explore one of those quintessentially Ally stress dreams—say, the one in which

> *"It is a truth universally acknowledged that every man in possession of a television set must be in love with Jenna Elfman or Calista Flockhart. Or both."*
>
> —*Olivia Goldsmith*, The New York Times

she forgets to file an important brief and gets fired. The rich pageant of anxiety would be broken only by the caterwauling of Morning Zoo deejays on Real McBeal's clock radio at the crack of dawn.

Excuse us if we prefer the Surreal McBeal.

Nope, Ally's world doesn't remotely resemble our own. Who would watch the show if it did? Ally's universe is a gleefully bizarro place populated by boogying twins, spear-chucking Mr. Huggy, and the seriously odd John Cage. Such loopy touches are a hallmark of writer/producer David Kelley, a former lawyer himself, the guy who practically invented the TV mutant known as the dramady (for greenhorns, that's a drama with comic touches, as exemplified by *L.A. Law* or *Picket Fences*, not a drama with comic touches that occasionally lurches into "very special" dramatic moments, like, um, *Blossom*).

It's not that *Ally McBeal* can't be serious, downbeat, even, (you remember Stephanie, the doomed transvestite?), but it's resolutely Not Real, and yes, all you prospective LSAT-takers at home, remember this disclaimer: Ally's job and real-life lawyering don't have much in common. (If you must endure a gritty lawyer show, there's always Kelley's earnestly yuck-free hour, *The Practice*.) *Ally McBeal* is the *Cop Rock* of lawyer shows, pure Courtroom of the Absurd. And we like it that way—we like it so much, we almost like lawyers while we're watching it. Allyworld is a quirky place with its own language, customs and fauna (see: neck wattles). So suspend disbelief, pack that briefcase and get ready for the grand tour.

Enter the famous unisex world of Ally McBeal

DOROTHY HANDELMAN

McBean Town

Love that dirty water! Not only is it cursed with the Red Sox, endless construction on the Central Artery, and the world's scariest drivers (Fox programmers, take note!), Boston must now contend with Hurricane McBeal.

Ally's a Boston girl—she attended Harvard Law School, works in an office that overlooks the city's financial district, and battles injustice (and myriad insecurities) in the grim corridors of the Suffolk County Courthouse. Heck, she's as Massachusetts as Faneuil Hall or the Old North Church.

Well, at least she's supposed to be. In reality, *Ally McBeal* is shot on some anonymous back lot in very un-Johnny Tremaine southern California (the Ren-Mar studios in Hollywood, actually, where *I Love Lucy* was filmed). But let's not split hairs. In spirit, anyway, this show is pure Bay State.

Why Boston? Before becoming a Hollywood megawriter, producer David Kelley was like Ally, a struggling young attorney in Beantown. As far as we know, that's where the similarities stop (reports that Kelley was squeezed on the *tuchus* at his first job simply cannot be verified). Here are some of Allyland's hot spots—nooks and crannies of the Massachusetts capital that have been featured on the show (or should have been, anyway):

5 Ally & Renee's Apartment (#3D), Beacon Hill

Since Ally loves to walk home from work in high heels (she's never so much as fingered a T token, let alone car keys), her neighborhood of choice would be tony Beacon Hill, which is just a hop, skip and a stumble in high heels from the courthouse.

4 Massachusetts College of Art, 621 Huntington Avenue

Care to join Ally and Renee in taking a sculpting class (or in ogling a well-endowed male model)? This is the place to do it.

3 Temple Kehillath Israel, Brookline

When Ally took on a client who couldn't get a "get" (Jewish divorce) from her comatose ex-husband, she wound up more than sparring with a certain Rabbi Stern. We have it on very, very good authority that this is his temple. Swear to…never mind.

2 The Combat Zone, Chinatown

Boston's seediest nook probably where John Cage would go trolling for hookers, and Ally's transvestite friend Stephanie met her untimely end.

1 Massachusetts Bar Association, 20 West Street

In the episode "One Hundred Tears Away" Ally gets hauled up before the state bar to answer charges that she is emotionally unstable. Who knew?

6 Harvard Law School, Cambridge

Go Crimson! Ally followed childhood sweetheart Billy Thomas to Harvard Law School, and when she made *Law Review* and he didn't, they broke up. Also branded with scarlet H's: Renee, Ally's best friend, and smarmy Richard Fish—Ally's future boss.

COURTESY OF THE STUART SELLARS/TRAVEL GRAPHICS INTL.

7 Cage/Fish & Associates, The Financial District

Judging from the panoramic opening shots used in nearly every episode, Ally's firm is right in the thick of the steel-and-glass thicket that makes up the city's financial district. Vonda Shepard's bar is said to be downstairs from the office.

8 The Public Garden

Okay, okay, we have no idea where Ally, Renee and Georgia pulled the infamous "Penguin Prank" on snowboarding Glenn, the artist's model. But since it happened in a place with a lot of trees, we took a wild stab and guessed it was here.

9 Suffolk County Courthouse, Pemberton Square

The austere facade of this building is glimpsed in nearly every episode of *Ally McBeal*. Location of Judge Whipper Cone's and Judge Happy Boyle's chambers.

10 US Justice Department, 99 Summer Street

When Janet Reno comes to town, this is where Fish heads to ogle the federal neck wattle.

11 Walpole State Penitentiary, Walpole

Ally says she's afraid of criminals, but two of her most memorable clients were cons: Michael Young, a lifer she helped get married (Ally was a bridesmaid at those cell block nuptials), and 78-year-old Vincent Robbins, who sprang himself from jail with a home-made trampoline.

12 The Hungry I, Beacon Hill

This romantic bistro is *the* place to come for a romantic date. Or a double date, like the disastrous outing shared by Ally, ex-boyfriend Ronald Cheanie, and Fish and Judge Whipper.

13 Hampshire House, Beacon Hill

No, not the location of Ally's favorite bar, but the bar *where everybody knows your name*...if you have the name of a Swedish tourist, that is. Just thought we'd mention it, but a chick as cool as Ally wouldn't be caught dead in here.

14 Caffe Vittoria, Hanover Street, the North End

This Italian coffeehouse has been whipping up Ally-licious cappuccinos in the Italian North End since the 1930's.

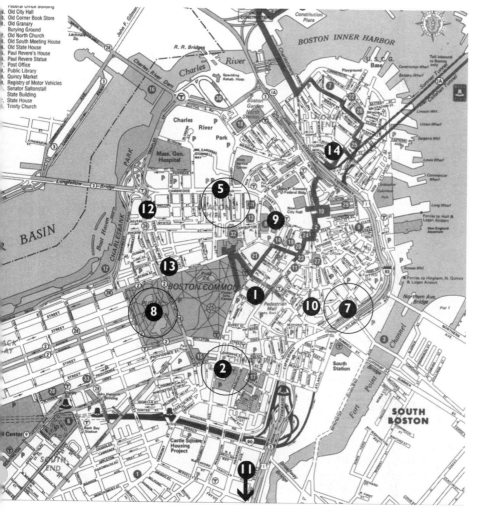

Flush This!

Used to be, toilets were the most unloved appliances on television. For years TV houses and offices came mysteriously unequipped with the porcelain buggers. Trips to the bathroom were practically unheard of; on the rare occasions TV characters did have to go, it was only to wash their hands. In the 1970s audiences were scandalized by the mere sound of Archie Bunker flushing, never mind seeing him using the famous commode.

Given that history of gun-shyness, the fact that *Ally McBeal*'s characters practically live in that spiffy lavender-and-gray co-ed loo is revolutionary. This is a john where characters not only drop their drawers, but their inhibitions. As Fish says, explaining his reasons for installing the Jack & Jill privy, "It helps men and women employees breed familiarity. So long as they don't come in and just breed."

We understand Fish's reasons for installing such an odd lavatory, but what about Ally creator David Kelley's reasons? The Unisexist inventor often says coyly that the idea came about simply because limited set space allowed the crew to construct just one bathroom. But he's also come up with some more plausible explanations: that the joint potty provided another spot where characters might run into each other, and that it was the perfect reflection of the personality of nosy, irrepressible Richard Fish. As Kelley explained to an audience at the Directors' Guild, building a unisex toilet fulfills the crafty founding partner's "lifelong quest to get into the ladies room."

Whatever its genesis, the Unisex isn't just the veritable corner-store of Allyworld—where Fish and Elaine go to eavesdrop and Cage wields his remote-control flusher (remember, he prefers a clean bowl)—it just may be the most talked about toilet in history. Don't think so? Check out these highlights from the history of the head and decide for yourself:

500 BC Palace of Minos in Crete is constructed with toilet in Queen's, um, *Megaron* (*Godzunheit!*) with sewer system underneath. Unfortunately plumber turns out to be surly half man, half beast who demands sacrifice of Athenian virgins as payment, launching industry tradition of exorbitantly high fees.

200s BC Greek inventor Archimedes discovers a method for determining the purity of gold while soaking in the tub. Shouts "Eureka," then runs amuck naked after making greatest bathroom-linked discovery until the face bra.

AD 500 In the Roman city of Timgad public pit toilets open to the street are constructed by BM-fixated inventor Marcus Fishicus.

AD 500-1000 Use of stinky, sloppy chamber pots make this the Toilet Dark Age. This is somewhat mitigated by the invention of the often not-stinky chambermaid, forerunner of bathroom lovin' lawyer Ally McBeal.

1793 Centuries-long taboo against co-ed bathrooms reinforced when French patriot Charlotte Corday, miffed by Jean-Paul Marat's prolonged soak in tub, stabs him repeatedly. Lesson reinforced in 1960, when Janet Leigh lingers too long in shower in *Psycho*.

1861 Thomas Crapper makes several innovations in the world of plumbing, turning name into punch line in process. (He was, however, never called the "Little Biscuit.")

1957 *Leave it to Beaver* is said to be the first show to depict an American bathroom, albeit one designed exclusively for applications of Dippity-Do.

1963 LBJ invents "multi-tasking" concept by meeting with White House staffers while using presidential commode.

1969 Nine people of both genders share a single bathroom—with no toilet—on the *Brady Bunch*. *Portnoy's Complaint* becomes bestseller, creating national sympathy for the three bathroom-deprived Brady Boys.

1971 Archie and Edith Bunker come down with stomach flu and run back-and-forth to john in groundbreaking episode that also introduces Edith's preachy, stomach-turning cousin, Maude.

1997 Richard Fish introduces Unisex to his law firm to breed familiarity. Winds up breeding familiarity with Judge Whipper Cone in toilet stall in the show's second episode, aptly entitled "Compromising Positions."

1998 Ally McBeal copes with ex-boyfriend's impending fatherhood by imagining lavatory floor show set to the cheesy Fifth Dimension classic "Wedding Bell Blues." Fortunately, rival's pregnancy turns out to be false alarm. Unfortunately ex-boyfriend catches Ally shaking her tail feather alone in the loo.

DOROTHY HANDELMAN

"If I were in a workplace that had a unisex bathroom, you wouldn't catch me dead in it."
—Calista Flockhart, *in* TV Guide

Kelley Girl

CHARLES W. BUSH/ SHOOTING STAR

docs-in-crisis hour *Chicago Hope*.

If you've been paying attention so far, you know that before Kelley found fortune in Hollywood, he was an attorney (he attended Princeton and Boston University law school). While a young associate at the firm Fine & Ambrogne, he scribbled off the film script that later became the forgettable 1987 lawyers-in-love comedy *From the Hip*, starring Brat Packer and future *Suddenly Susan* victim Judd Nelson.

Around the same time, the *From the Hip* script happened to cross the desk of TV drama pioneer Steven Bochco, creator of *Hill Street Blues*, who was looking for writers with legal knowledge to work on his new series, *L.A. Law*. Kelley signed on to write a single script and in short order became story editor and, eventually, executive producer. During his time at *L.A. Law*, Kelley scooped up five Emmys.

TV addicts may recall that the 1980s were a golden age of TV dramas—a time when shows from *St. Elsewhere* to *thirtysomething* revolutionized the medium by blurring the lines between the serious, wacky, gritty and—occasionally—the fantastic. Learning at the knee of Maestro Bochco, Kelley came of age as a writer and producer during this age of innovation. So it's not surprising that in 1989 he and his mentor would co-create another searing, critically acclaimed drama—*Doogie Howser, M.D.*

Ally wouldn't be Ally without David Kelley. She sprang, Athena-like, from the brow of one of television's most celebrated—and prolific— writers and producers. In *Ally McBeal*'s first season Kelley wrote every episode himself, as well as cranking out scripts for his ABC lawyer drama *The Practice* and producing the CBS

Doogie, you may remember, was a pimply prodigy who breezed through med school in, like, three weeks. Being both a kid and a genius kid doctor, Doogie was regularly forced to choose between the rigors of his medical residency and going to sock hops. Many people found Doogie warm family fun. Others thought the show (not to mention its name) ought to carry a warning label for diabetics.

But even if you adored Doogie, he was bush league entertainment next to Kelley's 1992 creation, *Picket Fences*, which explored life in tiny Rome, Wisconsin, a small town where very odd things had a way of happening.

Like *Ally McBeal*, *Fences* was instantly labeled a dramedy or a seriocomedy. It was by turns quirky, hilarious and very heavy. Characters invariably wound up bickering about Serious Issues such as abortion and euthanasia and airing their differences at the county courthouse. Critics loved the show, but audiences didn't. The series ran for four years on CBS, but in the end it proved no match for a competing show where strange things had a way of happening—the *X-Files*.

Calista Flockhart with Kathy Baker, who also appeared in Kelley's Picket Fences

Kelley Girl

After *Picket Fences*, Kelley created and produced the anti-*ER*, *Chicago Hope*, for the dowdy, angel-loving Tiffany network. Then in 1996, Fox came knocking—looking for a show to follow *Melrose Place* and run against *Monday Night Football*. The network gave Kelley creative carte-blanche, reportedly only asking for a "young franchise show that could incorporate humor and sex appeal." In other words, it had to be a show with mass quantities of Grrl Power.

Nobody questioned Kelley's genius, but there were those who wondered if a fortysomething rangy guy from the wilds of Maine could truly crawl into the head of a twentysomething female lead. Kelley has even joked that at the beginning of his research for *Ally McBeal*, he began reading *Cosmopolitan* —and couldn't believe the racy material behind that ubiquitous Scavullo cover shot. In the end Kelley decided not to try and write "women" (a concept that he says makes him "cringe") and to write interesting characters instead.

Ally, struggling Boston yuppie and incurable romantic, was born.

But casting Ally proved problematic. Originally Kelley pursued Bridget Fonda, but negotiations went nowhere. Scores of other young actresses read for the part, but none seemed to have the right blend of flightiness and intelligence that the role called for. Then Calista Flockhart arrived in Kelley's office, direct from New York. Kelley was instantly smitten, convinced that she embodied all things McBeal.

"I'm not Ally McBeal," Calista Flockhart once told reporters. "David insists that I am, but I'm not." But from the beginning observers were struck by how much Calista and Ally seemed to share besides great legs and bee-stung lips. In interviews, Flockhart was often endearingly spacey in a little-girl-lost kind of way—sort of like Ally when she delivered a eulogy for her dead professor and ex-lover in front of his widow and kids. Even though Flockhart was a seasoned Broadway trouper with a major motion picture hit under her belt (*The Birdcage*, with Robin Williams), she could come off, well, as kinda loopy. Maybe she was Ally—it really didn't matter. When the show debuted in September 1997, both were a hit.

When Kelley delivered the *Ally McBeal* pilot to Fox executives, he told them to brace for heat from those who wouldn't take kindly to a romantic comedy about a high-powered professional woman who felt incomplete without a man. Especially when that romantic comedy was written by a man. Indeed, *Entertainment Weekly* pointed out that for a chick show, *Ally McBeal* seemed concerned with a lot of classically male preoccupations, like prostitution and penis size. On the other hand, *Ally McBeal* managed to handle common female preoccupations, like commitment and motherhood anxiety, equally deftly. The result was not just a big hit, but another quirky Kelley original—a so-called chick show that also appealed to men.

After a smashing first season, critics have begun to wonder how long *Ally McBeal* can remain fresh and quirky without constant attention from its creator. Although he's cagey about when he'll hand off Ally writing chores to others, Kelley admits the time to surrender total creative con-

trol over his wunderkind is coming. Let's hope it's not too soon.

EVERETT COLLECTION; © 20TH-CENTURY FOX

It's Greek for "Most Beautiful"

When David Kelley accepted the 1997 Golden Globe award for best comedy series, he paid homage to "the little woman with the funny name." Calista Flockhart is used to being ribbed about her melodious, exotic moniker. In fact, as a kid she'd tell new friends her name was the familiar, all-American, easily pronounceable (and totally blah) Carol.

Luckily for us, she didn't make the change official. Here's the rest of the skinny on Miss Skinny:

THAT NAME

Is Greek for "Most Beautiful." Calista was named after her great-grandmother, who was named after a Roman Catholic saint. According to the baby-dubbing resource *The Last Word on First Names*, Calista is an "unfamiliar gem." (Yeah, right. With the show's success, you can bet little Calistas will be having play dates with fellow yuppie-guppie Emmas and Isabels before Ally goes into syndication . . .)

> *"So people think I'm lying about my age all the time? It's the records that are wrong. I've never once told anyone how old I am. The minute they ask me, I say, 'That's none of your business.' So that means I've never once lied about my age. Now that's true!"*
>
> —*Calista Flockhart, in* US

SETH POPPEL YEARBOOK ARCHIVES

> "I embrace everything about Ally . . . I don't particularly see her as a whiner. One week she's tough, the next she's really weak. I love that. She's human."
> —Calista Flockhart, in Entertainment Weekly

IT'S GREEK FOR "ALLY MCBEAL DOESN'T KNOW HOW LUCKY SHE IS"

Calista derives from the ancient Greek "Callisto," an ill-fated nymph who was raped and impregnated by Zeus, ostracized by former pal Artemis and then zapped into a big, woolly, flea-bitten bear. She now mopes about the heavens as Ursa Major.

A LITTLE DITTY 'BOUT JACK AND, ER, CALISTA

According to most sources (but not Calista, who gets huffy when reporters say she's 33), the future Ally McBeal was born on November 11, 1964, in the heartland backwater of Freeport, Illinois. Father Ronald was an executive for Kraft Foods while mom Kay was a schoolteacher. Because dad worked for the Cheez Whiz people, the family moved to rural Iowa, Minnesota and New Jersey during Calista's childhood.

GIMME A "C"

Calista spent her years in suburban Medford, New Jersey, and morphed into a teen queen. At Shawnee High School a more zaftig (perhaps it was all that American cheese?) Calista was a cheerleader, student council officer and a member of the "Shawnee Singers." This being New Jersey, she also had an amazingly fluffy Farrah hairdo.

THINK SHE'S STARVING NOW?

After graduating from Rutgers University in 1987, Calista headed to New York to be an actress (thea-tuh remains her first love). Though she worked steadily off-Broadway and in regional theater for seven years, she supplemented her income teaching aerobics. During the (ultra) lean year of 1993, she lived off a case of ravioli sent to her by older brother Gary.

CALISTA EXPLAINS IT ALL

Calista made her New York stage debut in the 1989 Circle Repertory production of (shades of things to come) "Beside Herself." Besides Calista, the play featured 11-year-old imp Melissa Joan Hart, of Clarissa Explains It All and Sabrina fame.

PLAYING THE ROLE OF THE GENTLEMAN CALLER TONIGHT, MISS JOAN VAN ARK!

Calista won acclaim for her 1994 Broadway debut as Laura in Tennessee Williams's "The Glass Menagerie," opposite Broadway legend Julie Harris (the crazy old bat on *Knot's Landing* to you and me). In 1996 she received praise and a Tony nod for her Natasha in an otherwise lambasted Chekov's "Three Sisters." Apparently costars Amy Irving, Jeanne Tripplehorn and Lili Taylor mistook "Three Sisters" for an episode of *Sisters*.

TWELVE STEPS TO SUCCESS

Calista appeared in a PBS film about the life of famed lawyer Clarence Darrow in 1991, then played an eating-disorder sufferer in the HBO movie *The Secret Life of Mary Margaret: Portrait of a Bulimic* and an alcoholic in the Showtime series *Drunks*. All of which prepared her for a career playing the world's most dysfunctional lawyer.

THE BIRD FROM BIRDCAGE

In 1996 Calista had a breakout role as the future daughter-in-law of gay couple Robin Williams and Nathan Lane in *The Birdcage*, a glossy remake of *La Cage aux Folles*. Other films she's appeared in: *Quiz Show*, *Milk Money*, and *Telling Lies in America*. Calista's just finished filming *A Midsummer Night's Dream*, with Kevin Kline and David Kelley's wife, Michelle Pfeiffer, and will star in the dark comedy *Like a Hole in the Head*.

MAIN SQUEEZE

The tabloids have linked Calista to actor Cedric Harris, Matt Damon and even happily-married-to-Michelle Pfeiffer David Kelley, but she dismisses such gossip as poppycock. It's been rumored that she's dating *Ally McBeal*'s co-executive producer, Jeffrey Kramer, but for now the only verifiable main man in Calista's life is Webster, a mixed-breed terrier.

IF CALISTA HAD A THEME SONG, IT WOULD BE . . .

Er, "Calista" by the Cuff Links, or maybe "The Greatest Love of All."

Clarista Flockhart appearing with Gene Hackman and Dianne Wiest in The Birdcage

Scorpio girl Calista insists she's not Ally McBeal, but the stars don't lie ... well, maybe they exaggerate a teensy-weensy bit. Scorpios fall deeply for their true loves and find breaking up hard to do (Billy, anyone?).

Astrology says she's a bit of a material girl, who likes to flaunt her assets in those leggy skirts (don't forget, under this ethereal waif lies the soul of a former aerobics instructor).

Calista Flockhart
Born: November 11, 1964
Freeport, Illinois
Sign: Scorpio

Calista's prone to "dreams, visions and longings"—in other words, she wouldn't have trouble conjuring up Mr. Huggy without David Kelley's help.

Not surprisingly for a filly who clawed her way from the Corn Belt to Hollywood, Calista's chart shows her to be driven and ambitious.

But an Aquarius moon betrays a quirky, hippy-dippy side. Guess Calista's right—she's not a *thing* like Ally.

29

(Re) Searchin' My Role

Maybe, as Billy says, Ally's a complete wacko. But sometimes she seems positively balanced next to the wackos she spends her time with. After getting her butt pinched one too many times at her first job, Ally took a job with her old law school nemesis, Richard Fish—a nattering nabob obsessed with making money. There she must cope not only with still loving her married ex-boyfriend, but actually liking his wife; fending off "help" from her passive-aggressive assistant, Elaine; and advances from weirdo founding partner John Cage. It's a wonder she ever makes it to court. Here's who's who in Allyworld:

GLOBE PHOTOS

ELAINE VASSAL (Jane Krakowski)
Job: Ally's assistant
Actual Job: Professional meddler, prodigious inventor
Hobbies: Gossip, volunteering sexual services
Quotable Quote: "Snappish!" (when Ally is being, well, snappish)
Role Model: Theodora, She-bitch of Byzantium
Theme Song: "Heard It Through the Grapevine"

BILLY ALLEN THOMAS (Gil Bellows)
Job: Fellow associate at the firm
Actual Job: Ex-boyfriend, shoulder to cry on
Hobbies: Slow dancing with no music, apologizing
Quotable Quote: "You're the woman I want to spend my life with, Georgia."
Role Model: Phil Donahue
Theme Song: "Torn Between Two Lovers"

RENEE RADICK (Lisa Nicole Carson)
Job: Deputy district attorney
Actual Job: Ally's best friend and rock of emotional stability, doler out of Tough Love
Hobbies: Kickboxing
Quotable Quote: (to Ally) "You're an emotional idiot."
Role Models: Jean Claude Van Damme, Dr. Laura
Theme Song: "Kung Fu Fighting"

RICHARD FISH (Greg Germann)
Job: Founding partner at the firm
Actual Job: Making Fishisms, eavesdropping
Hobbies: Making money, fingering neck wattles, Cohiba cigars
Quotable Quote: "Bygones."
Role Models: Machiave[lli], Gordon Gecko
Theme Song: "Mone[y] (That's What I Want[)]"

JUDGE JENNIFER "WHIPPER" CONE, AKA THE WHIPPER (Dyan Cannon)
Job: Respected jurist
Actual Job: Fiftysomething sexpot, object of Richard Fish's wattle worship
Hobbies: Making law, making whoopee and color rinses
Quotable Quote: "It's not that you're sick, Richard; it's just that you're sick. And by the time you get well, I could be dead."
Role Model: Tina Turner
Theme Song: "Afternoon Delight"

THE DANCING TWINS (Eric and Steve Cohen)
Job: Dancing Twins
Actual Job: Dancing Twins
Hobbies: Um, dancing (with Renee and Ally when they don't have dates)
Quotable Quote: "Shut up and dance, already."
Role Model: David Cassidy (clothes, moves)
Theme Song: "It Takes Two"

GEORGIA THOMAS (Courtney Thorne-~~~h)

~~~sociate at firm,
~~~ife of Billy
~~~h: Making Ally
~~~y being won-
~~~y way
~~~ nice,
~~~ husband

~~~ to
~~~ Billy

JOHN CAGE, AKA THE BISCUIT, THE LITTLE BISCUIT, OR DOUGHBOY (Peter MacNicol)
Job: Co-founder of firm with Fish; he was to be the "pillar of dignity"; Fish was to be "the shark."
Actual Job: Village oddling
Hobbies: Taking moments, smile therapy, using remote-control toilet flusher, soliciting the occasional prostitute
Quotable Quote: "I'm ~~~roubled."
~~~le Model: The boy ~~~e bubble
~~~e Song: "Space

THE SINGER (Vonda Shepard)
Job: Singer at Ally's after-work watering hole
Actual Job: Sings every song used in the show, *slowly*
Hobbies: Soul searchin'
Quotable Quote: "Is it me, or does this microphone smell like a beer?"
Role Models: Aretha Franklin or Susan Anton; depends on the song
Theme Song: "Piano Man"

JUDGE DENNIS "HAPPY" BOYLE (Phil Leeds)
Job: Semi-respected jurist
Actual Job: Resident tooth fetishist
Hobbies: Checking the dental work of lawyers who appear before him
Quotable Quote: "Let's see your teeth."
Role Model: The Osmonds
Theme Song: "Smile"

~~~RD" (Baby Cha-cha)

~~~ticking biological clock
~~~n' jiggy with it

~~~ Rosemary's Baby,

EVERETT C~~~ HOWARD ROSENBERG/SHOOTING STAR SATORI/SHOOTING STAR

Michelle McBeal

More than a few commentators have noticed an eerie resemblance between sensuous-mouthed, sorta-blond actress Calista Flockhart and sensuous-mouthed, sorta-blond actress Michelle Pfeiffer, who just happens to be married to *Ally McBeal* producer David Kelley. A few tabloids hinted that Kelley was taking more than a professional interest in his doe-eyed star, a virtual replica of his still doe-eyed but, well, slightly longer-in-the-tooth wife (the *New York Daily News* later reported that the rumors were the result of a misunderstanding—she was actually dating Kelley's partner, Jeffrey S. Kramer, but the pair were keeping the relationship secret because he was newly separated).

Meanwhile both Flockhart and Kelley say they were never struck by any similarity to Pfeiffer. "I find it hugely flattering," Flockhart told *TV Guide*. "I feel like I have to apologize to her." Perhaps she already has—the pair will soon appear together in a new film version of *A Midsummer Night's Dream*. Sorry, news from the set was that the dopplegangers got on amicably.

Maybe the resemblance hasn't been overstated. After all, Michelle Pfeiffer is a birdlike, gorgeous, talented movie actress and Flockhart is a birdlike, gorgeous, talented television star. Not so sure? Use the handy Calista/Michelle/Melista/Cachelle comparison chart on the next page:

PAUL FENTON/SHOOTING STAR

MICHAEL FERGUSON/GLOBE PHOTOS

MICHELLE PFEIFFER

Age: 40?

Hair Color: Brownish Blond

Adolescent Highlight: Miss Orange County (cried when crowned)

Character-Building White Trash Work Experience: Supermarket checkout girl

Early TV Exposure: Worked with strange, enigmatic Mr. Roarke on *Fantasy Island*

Musical Comedy: Upstaged by preening pretty boy Adrian Zmed in *Grease 2*

Chemical Dependency: Depended on Mel Gibson in *Tequila Sunrise*

Vonda Shepard, Watch Your Back: Sang lounge chestnut "You're Just Too Good to Be True" in *The Fabulous Baker Boys*

Struck Blow for Grrl Power by: Joining forces with Susan Sarandon to zap Jack Nicholson in *The Witches of Eastwick*

Ally McBeal-est Moment: Attractive single villainess Catwoman is plagued by feelings of insecurity when forced to work with old flame Batman in *Batman Returns*

CALISTA FLOCKHART

Age: 33?

Hair Color: Blondish brown

Adolescent Highlight: Made cheerleader (cried when home team lost)

Character-Building White Trash Work Experience: Aerobics instructor

Early TV Exposure: Worked with strange, enigmatic Kevin Spacey in *Darrow*

Musical Comedy Work: Upstaged by preening not-so-pretty boy Nathan Lane in *The Birdcage*

Chemical Dependency: Depended on tequila in the cable flick *Drunks*

Vonda Shepard, Call Your Lawyer: Sang lounge chestnut "Searchin' My Soul"—off-key—in an episode of *Ally McBeal*

Struck Blow for Grrl Power by: Joining forces with Susan Sarandon to zap Bosnian rapists at a benefit stage presentation of Eve Ensler's *The Vagina Monologues*

Cat Woman-est Moment: Bad girl Ally McBeal called a "man-eater" after accepting two dates, one of which is with an actual *rabbi*—and heavens, she's a Methodist. Rrrrrowr!

Ally The Jury

We've already pointed out that some sour grapes in the legal community think *Ally McBeal* legal work is pure *Fantasy Law-land*. "It's totally ridiculous," gripes Antonia More, a 37-year-old attorney in Oakland, California. "They seem to take cases that frankly, from a business point of view, are bottom feeder law—it's all family, personal injury and criminal defense work—and yet they have these swanky offices and a staff of 50 to help just 5 lawyers."

You'd think as a former lawyer, David Kelley would know better. But then he probably realizes that a show about what most lawyers actually do for a living would send viewers into irreversible boredom-induced comas. And anyway, what really cheeses many lawyers off about *Ally McBeal* isn't that it distorts what lawyering is all about, but that it does something far worse—it actually makes lawyering look *fun*.

Big surprise: It isn't. Or as one lawyer puts it, "Ally doesn't have any homework." Well, now *you* do—here are some popular attorney slams at *Ally McBeal*. Save this list for a Monday night, whip out the Jiffy Pop, and ruin the show for friends!

> *"I wouldn't hire her for my attorney."*
>
> —Susan Carroll, a 32-year-old New York lawyer, in Entertainment Weekly

> *"When Ally gets any work done, how she keeps her job, why she thinks it's okay to ask her secretary why she didn't give her a birthday present—these are all mysteries."*
>
> —Gina Bellafante, Time

1. **THOSE OFFICES:** Okay, these digs are the headquarters of a law firm started by a thirtysomething barely out of tort class? Even if Fish is independently wealthy (possible), this glossy operation is hemorrhaging around $15,000 a month in rent.

2. **COULD YOU AND YOUR SIXTEEN FRIENDS MAKE A COPY OF THE LEWINSKY FILE?:** Are the scores of people milling about at the firm employed for anything but dance routines? There are only five lawyers in the whole place, and 800 secretaries.

3. **PAULA JONES, DO WE HAVE A FIRM FOR YOU:** Let's get this straight—in less than a year Georgia, Ally, and Elaine have all made sexual harassment complaints? At least at Tailhook you got a chance to shoot craps . . .

4. **SPEEDY GONZALEZ, PRESIDING:** In the real world jury trials take more than 15 minutes to solve. A case would not go before a court of appeal lickety-split—the process may take years. Even busy trial lawyers are lucky to have a handful of court cases a year, not one a week.

5. **HAND IN THAT GAVEL:** Ally reaches new heights of absurdity in the judge department. A jurist who insists on seeing lawyers' teeth and who patronizes hookers? Another who lets her boyfriends' employees try cases in her courtroom without recusing herself? This is Boston, not Babylon.

6. **DID SOMEBODY MENTION TAILHOOK?:** More unlawyerly sexual shenanigans: The firm actively encourages Ally to date client Ronald Cheanie, senior partner John Cage asks Ally out, husband and wife Georgia and Billy work together without a flurry of concern, associates speak openly about lawyers soliciting prostitutes, and we haven't even started on Elaine . . .

7. **SUE ME? YOU'LL GET THE CHAIR!:** Cage/Fish & Associates, supposedly a civil law firm (Fish thinks criminal law is skuzzy) regularly find themselves in criminal courts. Murder? Divorce? Wrongful termination? Legal wunderkind Ally's your girl. Well, she did go to Harvard . . .

8. **WE WARNED YOU ABOUT THE SKIRTS:** The dress code—what dress code?

9. **WHAT IS THIS, A LAW FIRM OR STUDIO 54?:** The Unisex. You know why.

10. **LIKE WE SAID, NO HOMEWORK:** Seems these barflies go out every night—are they drinking club soda in those martini glasses? And when they're not throwing one back before important court cases, Ally and Renee still find time to take a sculpture class.

Gals of Justice

Despite devious attempts by the patriarchy to suppress their accomplishments, women have long made substantive and important contributions to the law. There's no doubt we've come a long way since poor Justice was forced to wear that duvet-and-blindfold number. As the chart below illustrates, Ally McBeal, Esq. is just the latest in a long line of female legal pioneers:

Legal Pioneer: Portia of Venice
Greatest Triumph: Saved Antonio from evil money-lender Shylock
Resume: Speak and write Italian. Adept at cross-dressing. Board-certified plague free.
Fashion Tip: A pound of flesh goes with everything.
Courtroom Wisdom: If you find the quality of mercy strained, trick the bastards.

Legal Pioneer: Bella Abzug
Greatest Triumph: Brassy congresswoman championed women's rights
Resume: Can shatter glass with voice; has Gloria Steinem on speed dial.
Fashion Tip: You can leave your hat on.
Courtroom Wisdom: If all else fails, an impromptu bra burning is good for laughs.

Legal Pioneer: Sandra Day O'Connor
Greatest Triumph: First woman appointed to Supreme Court
Resume: Winner, Flagstaff Jane Wyman Look-alike Contest, 1945.
Fashion Tip: Senate Judiciary Committees prefer blondes.
Courtroom Wisdom: Note to self: never share Pepsi with Clarence Thomas.

Trendsetter: Lani Guinier
Greatest Triumph: Wrote bestseller after being passed over for Equal Employment Opportunity Commission post
Resume: Politburo Chair, Yale Black Liberation Dashiki Collective, 1971
Fashion Tip: Who says Afro-Puffs went out of style?
Courtroom Wisdom: Never again, under any circumstances, utter the word "quota."

Trendsetter: Ruth Bader Ginsberg
Greatest Triumph: Second woman on Supreme Court; keyed Antonin Scalia's car.
Resume: Winner, Flatbush Ruth Buzzi Look-alike Contest, 1975.
Fashion Tip: Nothing softens your look like a severe bun and thick black glasses.

Courtroom Wisdom: Good justices come in small packages.

Trendsetter: Janet Reno
Greatest Triumph: First woman attorney general
Resume: Can kill, clean and dress gator in 15 minutes.
Fashion Tip: No outfit is complete without a subpoena.
Courtroom Wisdom: Never let a strange man finger your neck wattle.

Attorney General Janet Reno

Trendsetter: Ally McBeal
Greatest Triumph: Having a "less bad" day
Resume: Have emotional baggage, catchy theme song. Will travel.
Fashion Tip: Any skirt less than six inches above the knee is unprofessional.
Courtroom Wisdom: Love and law are the same, romantic in concept, but the actual practice can get you a yeast infection.

Allyisms Allyisms

Unfamiliar with Ally McBeal-speak? Curious about the origin of the nickname "The Biscuit," befuddled by "bygones"? Peruse this miniglossary of Ally terms:

Barbie and Midge; Barbie and Skipper: Dolls for which, respectively, Georgia and Ally are often mistaken.

The Biscuit (or the Little Biscuit): Nickname for John Cage, strangoid senior partner at Ally's firm. It seems that in high school doughy little John bore some resemblance to the Pillsbury Doughboy and, according to series creator David Kelley, was frequently "poked and prodded" by his peers. Contrary to popular lore, the name has nothing to do with his sexual organs or the slang term for a hockey puck.

Bygones: Term used by Richard Fish and adopted by his colleagues, it roughly translates to "water under the bridge." As in: "Killed her husband, slipped her mind—it happens! By-gones!"

Clean Bowl: What John Cage prefers in visit to the bathroom. In order to guarantee a clean bowl, Cage carries a remote-control device that allows him to flush a toilet from a distance—and not be greeted by any unpleasant surprises—when he opens the stall door.

Cool Cup: Fertility device invented by Elaine Vassal. An ice-cold jockstrap worn to increase sperm count.

Face Bra: Invention patented by Elaine Vassal. A bandagelike contraption with an opening for the eyes that holds the face in place while jogging, preventing pulling that can cause wrinkles. Ally commented that when wearing the face bra, Elaine looks like "Hannibal Lecter."

Fishism: Snarky, self-serving platitudes served up by Richard Smith, such as, "It's not about winning, it's winning ugly that matters."

Human Window of Opportunity: Nickname given to Elaine by fellow classmates during her "free-and-easy" period in high school.

Husband CD: Another quirky Elaine Vassal invention, this is a recording, designed for single women, of all the sounds found in a spousal relationship, including belching, flatulence and a televised football game.

Ice Goggles: Invented by—you guessed it—Elaine Vassal, these glasses packed with ice shrink puffiness around the eyes after a hard night of partying.

McBealism: An often self-deprecating observation on life and love made by Ally McBeal, as in: "Whoever said that plenty of fish in the sea thing was lying. Sometimes there's only one fish. Trust me." In spirit, often the polar opposite of a Fishism.

EVERETT COLLECTION: © 20TH-CENTURY FOX

Allyisms Allyisms

Mr. Not Likely: Man Ally decides to date even though she knows the possibility of a long-term relationship is slim. Glenn, the snowboarding artist's model, and Rabbi Stern, with whom she shares her sharp tongue but little else, are two examples.

A Moment: A public moment of silence frequently employed by John Cage during trials, used to collect thoughts and unnerve the opposition.

The Penguin: Prank invented by Ally and Renee at Harvard Law School. One of the pair lures a deserving man to a supposedly private spot and induces him to drop his drawers and waddle after her, aroused, trousers around his ankles. This penguinlike action is captured for posterity by the coconspirator, and the victim is left stranded—and publicly humiliated.

Poughkeepsie: Word used by John Cage when he feels an attack of nerves coming on. When on the spot, Cage stutters, but saying "Poughkeepsie" while humming and muttering calms him.

Snappish!: Term used by Elaine to describe those—especially Ally—who show displeasure with her busybody ways.

Snappish Stereo: Same as above when employed by two people at same time, e.g., Ally and Billy showing displeasure with Elaine's busybody ways.

Allyisms Allyisms

Stomach Gurgle: Another of Cage's nervous tics. In order to avoid detection he has learned to throw his stomach gurgle across a room like a ventriloquist throws her voice.

Swish: What Cage says Ally does with her hands as she talks in court—waving them about while trying to make a point, which actually undermines it. As in, "You swish your hands."

The Unisex: Slang for the coed toilet at Cage/Fish & Associates.

Waffle: What Cage senses in Ally after she accepts his request for a date. Second thoughts, particularly in the romance department.

Wattle: Wrinkly, drooping flesh below a woman's chin that grows more pronounced with age. Richard Fish is sexually aroused by fingering women's wattles—especially those of Whipper and her rival, Attorney General Janet Reno. He once lost control and touched Georgia's incipient wattle but later apologized.

Whipper: Nickname for Judge Jennifer Cone, origin unclear. Creator David Kelley has said the nickname just seemed to sum up the lusty, take-charge jurist. This is one kitten who knows her way around a whip . . .

She's Got Person

A Day in the Life of Ally McBeal

> *"The show came to England the week I came to America [for a book tour for* Bridget Jones's Diary.*] I've seen one episode, and I loved it . . . I think Ally's much thinner than Bridget, though."*
>
> —*Helen Fielding, author of the very Ally-esque* Bridget Jones's Diary

Believe it or not, 1998 won't merely be remembered as the year of *Ally McBeal*. A couple of other fairly newsworthy things happened—India and Pakistan exploded nuclear devices, a saucy intern with a thing for berets turned the White House upside down and Celine Dion assaulted the world with a maudlin ballad about a sinking cruise ship.

But perhaps the most interesting event, in Ally-terms, anyway, was the rise of a transatlantic female phenomenon with a tad more depth than the Spice Girls. Her name was Bridget Jones and in spirit, she was very much the limey Ally McBeal.

Bridget began life as the fictional author of a column in London's *Independent* newspaper, then morphed into the heroine of a bestselling novel. In diary-entry form, Bridget chronicles her misadventures as a swinging single gal in swinging London town. Loosely based on the heroine of *Pride and Prejudice* (did somebody say Jane Austen? Call Hollywood!), Bridget Jones reminded American reviewers immediately not of Elizabeth Bennet, but of a certain chronically insecure Boston lawyer.

Like Ally, Bridget was a slightly out-there romantic lost in the modern world—fond of very short skirts and long interior monologues. And like Ally, she drew strong reaction—some British women thought her their mirror, others were horrified by her perceived wimpiness. British men found her spunky and endearing, and on the other big V-day, hundreds of lonely characters actually

> *"The British best-seller is a literary Ally McBeal. A new genre—the lack of romance novel."*
>
> —*Jim Mullen's Hot Sheet,* Entertainment Weekly

> *"It's like we're plugged into the same cosmic Zeitgeist. I mean here we are, these two virtual twins who like to wear short skirts: two babes if I say so myself, with good legs, a good sense of humor and bad boyfriends."*
>
> —*Michiko Kakutani impersonating Ally McBeal writing a letter to soulmate Bridget Jones in* The New York Times

Ally-ty

sent Bridget *valentines*.

Rampant Bridgetmania is the last thing Ally's self-esteem needs. Of course, if Ally had the time to write a diary in between fantasies, dating disasters and court cases, she'd get thousands of valentines, too. And not anemic, puny, ironic little English valentines, either. No, she'd receive loads of red-blooded, robust, manly-man all-American cards. So, in the interest of evening the score, here's a look at Ally McBeal's diary (well, what her Filofax would look like if she kept one, anyway—after all, she's a busy girl).

SEPTEMBER
21 MONDAY

7:00 A.M. Rise to the pounding sound of Renee's kickboxing exercises; ponder why I occasionally find her aura of good health, emotional stability such a downer. Can self-flagellation be considered a form of exercise?

7:30 A.M. Eat Jell-O for breakfast in my favorite oversized pair of Nick & Nora pajamas with the sheep motif, the ones with the too-long arms that flop over my hands, so instead of looking like I'm twelve I look like I'm seven. Ignore dancing baby on way to shower. He knows the rules - no frigging dancing until after work.

8:00 A.M. Decide what to wear - either the lavender jacket and matching miniskirt or the gray-blue jacket and matching miniskirt. Both go with my stacked heels (perfect for that big murder trial). Decide against matching neckerchief. Makes me feel like a Pan Am stewardess from 1975 or, worse, Mary Tyler Moore. Ugh.

21 MONDAY

8:15 A.M. Walk to work; lose myself in reverie about meaning of love. Is there really only one person for everyone? If so, does that mean that Billy's made a mistake in marrying Georgia, or maybe it's that Georgia's his right person and she's his, and I'm just this sort of dysfunctional extra person who was accidentally programmed by God or something to love Billy forever? Or maybe there are two right people for every person, and out there somewhere — I don't know, maybe in Detroit, even, there's my Georgia — I mean George. Wait, do I find Georgia attractive? Is that why I keep self-destructing on all these blind dates? Make a note for Dr. Clark. Did I make a mistake about the neckerchief? (Momentarily interrupt interior monologue to berate man who accidentally bumps into me.)

- **8:30 A.M.** Stop for supremely frothy cappuccino. Imagine self swimming in froth with some mysterious, swarthy Colombian coffee-picking-type guy. Not Billy. Repeat, not Billy.

- **9:00 A.M.** Get messages from Elaine. Avoid small talk with Elaine by barreling straight ahead into my office. Remember, eye contact only encourages her. Twirl about once in big, squishy office chair and soak in eye-popping view of Boston. Not bad for a 28-year-old who's afraid of criminals.

- **9:30 A.M.** Meeting with new client in conference room. Want to tell Richard I have Epstein-Barr or I've been kidnapped by the Symbionese Liberation Army. Anything to get out of it. I can feel myself shrinking, becoming smaller and smaller in the conference room. Meetings like that make me feel like I'm 10 — like it's take-myself-to-work day or something.

21 MONDAY

10:45 A.M. Head for bathroom break in order get over trauma of having to sit through the meeting I'll be too much of a trouper to refuse to go to. Sometimes I hate myself for actually biting the bullet and doing the grown-up thing. I mean, I'd much rather be irresponsible and sit in my office and color or something, but then I guess I'd lose my job – and all my neckerchiefs! Anyway, I actually like being a lawyer most of the time; it's just that I don't want to be just this lawyer-person all the time. I'd rather be a person-person. Interrupt this reverie to check bathroom stalls to make sure Elaine or Richard isn't hiding in them or that I get so lost in my thoughts I back into the stall without looking and accidentally sit on Georgia's lap again. That was so humiliating and yet so comforting. Sitting on her lap felt like being a little girl. She's so strong and nurturing and pretty – God, I hate her. Make sure to discuss with Dr. Clark.

DOROTHY HANDELMAN

- 10:46 A.M. Run into Billy in bathroom, into Georgia in bathroom, into Fish and Elaine in bathroom. Discuss the new client from the conference meeting with everybody. Wonder what their kink will be. Knowing this place, they'll be really out there - like a cross-dressing necrophiliac who wants to be officially married to his favorite corpse or a woman whose family wants to commit her because she thinks she channels the 12 apostles. Ah, well, I'm sure they'll initially gross me out, but in a half hour or so I'll dis-cover - and even relate to - their innate humanity. In any case, I'm sure their quirky problem will provide a nice springboard for me to get in touch my own feelings. It's been so long.

- 11:00 A.M. Expect John Cage to enter Unisex by flushing toilet with his remote-control thingy. Allow him time for one truly strange observation, and say something about the reso-nance of the flush or his ability to throw his stomach growls across the room. Then leave the bathroom with everybody else. Boy, can that guy clear a room.

21 MONDAY

11:30 A.M. See Billy in hallway. Drag him back into my office and force him to give me pep talk along these lines: "Ally, you are not flighty. It's just that you feel more intensely than other people do. You're a wacko, but you're also a true romantic, and I wouldn't have it any other way." Hug. Turn around in mock surprise when Georgia walks in (God, I love that). Make awkward conversation; get annoyed when Elaine pokes fat head in. Deny being snappish as I shoo everybody out. Trip and fall on way to desk. Imagine I'm trying to keep from drowning in an enormous vat of lavender-gray-blue Jell-O. Why is it that I'm always the one getting hurt in my fantasies – shoving my foot in my mouth, getting tossed in the Dumpster, getting shot with arrows, swimming too far underwater? Why can't I ever dream myself up an Uzi and take out all these annoying people? Make note of this for Dr. Clark.

- **12:20 P.M.** Lunch! I've been working so hard on myself by this point that I may run a little late. Meet Renee at the courthouse for two low-fat Pringles. (Well, I'll eat that; she'll have a hamburger and still look good). Discuss day so far with Renee; brace self for her obvious criticism — that I'm too self-absorbed. Duh. I love being self-absorbed. If I weren't, I wouldn't be me. I'd be some weird fem-bot version of me. Miss Nicey-Nicey on the outside and nothing on the inside, like, uh, those Russian dolls that fit inside each other, and they're pretty but you keep peeling away the layers and there's nothing there. I'd be . . . Georgia. Make note for Dr. Clark.

21 MONDAY

1:30 P.M. Stay at courthouse to meet friend of Renee's from the DA's office. He's possible date material, a real prime slice of man-meat. I only hope he won't have any horrible habits, like spitting when he talks, or smelling his food really obviously before he eats it, or, I don't know, breathing too hard through his mouth. It's so hard to find that perfect person when you know there really probably is only one, and that he's married to a woman you swear you really like, but you wouldn't really mind if she'd, say, wind up in an iron lung or a plastic bubble or something. I mean, I don't want to hurt Georgia - got that out of my system during our kick-boxing match. I just want her off in some contained space where she can't barge in on me and Billy during our heart-to-hearts. Someplace like . . . prison.

2:00 P.M. After meeting new guy, remember other reason for being at courthouse - the murder trial! Try to overcome feelings of dread and revulsion for criminals - oops - I mean criminal defendants - no, wait, that's not what I mean - oh, forget it. I just hope I can do a good job for my client, Crusher Gravelli. I mean, maybe he did-n't really mean to strangle his ex-wife's husband; maybe it just sort of happened. I've wanted to strangle Elaine lots of times. And really, I'm sure there's a warm, wounded side to this killer - um, I mean defendant, because, well, there always is. I just can't figure out how this case relates to my problems. I just know there's got to be a connection somewhere.

5:00 P.M. Verdict should be in by now, so I'll probably start walking back to the office, thinking about what it all meant to me. Maybe I'll ask that cute prosecutor on the case out for coffee. That couldn't hurt. I mean, he's totally wrong for me; he's got this beauty mark on his left eyelid that's so dis-tracting - I mean, is this Mr. Not Likely or what - but he's funny and smart, and I know it's wrong to have been flirting with him during the trial, but it was just unstoppable animal magnetism. Make note of this for Dr. Clark. Magnetism. If he goes out for coffee with me, I hope that damn baby doesn't show up again on in-line skates, or in a wrestling unitard or a kendo outfit or something. I can't take him pestering.

8 P.M. Meet Renee, Richard, Georgia, Billy, Elaine, Whipper and John for drinks at the bar. I wonder what Vonda Shepard will be singing tonight - probably some old Burt Bacharach tune or something that was number #15 on the charts in 1973. Sometimes I wish she'd crank out some Pearl Jam or Hole. I mean, I wasn't even born when most of the songs she sings were written. I'm only 28, after all - "Thriller" is an oldie to me. I said, I'm only 28. Really. May my breasts - er - my nose - grow if I'm lying. Oh, now I'll have to wait for my fantasy nose to shrink. Damn!

11:00 P.M. Walk back to apartment with Renee arm-in-arm. Discuss dating pluses and minuses of both her friend, the DA, and my friend and opposing counsel DA. At least her friend doesn't have that eye-freckle thing. Just saying that makes me imagine his birthmark growing larger and larger until it blots out half of his face like a port-wine stain. I sound so shallow. Look, it's not that I hate eye freckles, it's just that I think if you are going to spend time with someone, they better meet some basic Billy — sorry! I meant basic standards of attractiveness. I mean, what's the point otherwise? Let's face it, I'm a dish; I deserve Bil — perfection. Discuss with Dr. Clark.

SEPTEMBER

21 MONDAY

11:59 P.M. Put on Nick & Nora pajamas, eat comforting bowl of Jell-O, let rays of pearly moonlight pour into my darkened bedroom and start shimmying with Mr. Huggy to the song "I Only Want to Be With You." But not the catchy Dusty Springfield version, the slow, melancholy, very me-'n'-Vonda version. Flit about until suitably groggy, then head off to sleep. That's the one time I never seem to dream, thank goodness – should I mention that to Dr. Clark?

Don't Walk Away, Renee!

Having someone as high-maintenance as Ally McBeal for a best friend isn't a job for the faint of heart. Luckily, Ally's got deputy DA—and master kickboxer—Renee Radick in her corner. Not only is Renee gorgeous and intelligent, she's the one character on *Ally McBeal* who truly has her act together—if she caught that animated baby skulking around her bedroom, she wouldn't dance with him, she'd kick him into next week. And where men are concerned, Renee is self-assured and pragmatic; she's not pining away for anybody (well, she did have a little crush on John Cage, of all people). All things considered, Renee's the anti-Ally.

Renee's strength was no accident. David Kelley didn't want the character to fall into the "Rhoda" model of sitcom B.F.'s (think someone dotty, man-hungry, and insecure; think *fat jokes*). Since Ally was already dotty, man-hungry and insecure, her buddy had to be a rock—the kind of person who would give her the advice she didn't want to hear and tell her straight up when she was making a fool of herself.

Good thing he cast Lisa Nicole Carson in the part—she's an actress who naturally radiates a beguiling combo of wit and warmth. She's so good, she almost makes you want to utter that cursed word: spin-off. But then, who would Ally turn to?

"The opportunities to get out of [the "sassy black woman" stereotype] are so few and far between, I just really want to relish the moment."
—Lisa Nicole Carson, *in* Entertainment Weekly

STRAIGHT OUTTA BROOKLYN

Lisa was born in 1970 in the Vinnie Barbarino borough and raised in New York City and Florida. She began acting professionally as a youngin' at the City Kids Rep and Playwrites Horizons of New York.

SHE'S ALWAYS CRABBY

A Cancer, Lisa is rumored to have a sexy crab tattoo on her stomach.

WHAT A YENTA

In grade school, Lisa got bitten by the theater bug after being cast as the matchmaker in "Fiddler on the Roof." But, as she told USA Today, even then she craved center stage. "I wanted to be Tevye," Carson said. "I wanted to be all his daughters at once. I knew everybody's line, everybody's inflections. I wanted to sing 'Sunrise, Sunset' so badly it was killing me."

WHAT A YENTL

Although she's sung both rock and R&B professionally, Lisa's idol is the schmoozy Barbra Streisand—she has said she'd like to model her career on that of the singing, acting, directing, fingernail-buffing superstar. Sounding a little like her diva heroine, she once declared, "I'm unable to ignore the gift that God gave me, and so I'm going to sing." (Incidentally, Carson appeared in a short-lived Fox series called Divas, and performed briefly with Mascara, an all-female rock band). Although she has sung on Ally McBeal, there is as yet no Color Me Lisa Nicole in stores.

SUDDENLY CAST LISA

Lisa worked on the New York stage, appearing in productions at the Westbeth and Negro Ensemble theater companies, among others. Like Martin stars Tichina Arnold and Tisha Campbell, she was featured as a Supremes-style backup singer in a production of Little Shop of Horrors. In 1999 Lisa will also star with Eddie Murphy and the not cute-Ally-wacko but just plain wacko comic Martin Lawrence in the movie Life.

WE LET LISA BONET SPEAK, AND LOOK WHAT HAPPENED

Lisa's television debut happened to be a walk-on part on the final episode of The Cosby Show in 1992. After she tried to ad-lib, she was warned not to say a word by the assistant director. She tried to compensate by contorting her face into various dramatic expressions (and this was years before John Cage tried smile therapy). Someone must have thought they were hysterical, because shortly thereafter Lisa was a regular on a short-lived def-jam comedy sketch series The Apollo Comedy Hour.

JADA'S LYRIC

While other stars of The Apollo Comedy Hour went back to their day jobs (whither cast mate "Kool Bubba Ice"?), in 1994 Lisa snagged a role in the violent inner-city love story Jason's Lyric, which starred Jada Pinkett. She then achieved every girl's dream by appearing opposite Denzel Washington in Devil in a Blue Dress, followed by a role in the Ally-McBeal-goes-buppie comedy Love

Jones. In 1997 Lisa appeared in the critically acclaimed sleeper *Eve's Bayou* with Junee Smollett, Lynn Whitfield, Samuel Jackson and Victoria Rowell—who appears on the cheesy soap *The Young and the Restless* and the even cheesier Depends-set mystery *Diagnosis Murder*.

DOUBLE TROUBLE

Like Rowell, Lisa has two day jobs—but neither are cheesy. Since 1996 she has appeared irregularly on *ER* as strong-willed Carla Reese, the mother of icy surgeon Dr. Peter Benton's love child. Since *Ally McBeal*'s premiere she has continued to work on both shows.

DROP THOSE CRUTCHES!

Since joining the Fox family, Lisa's picked up some interesting habits: smoking cigars and guzzling fruit shakes. "It was everything: protein, energy, nicotine," the un-health-conscious Carson commented. However, she's determined to change her ways for *Ally*'s second season: "I've just been bouncing from crutch to crutch to crutch, so this summer I'm working on no crutches. I want to walk on my own." Does this mean she'll move from kickboxing to X-treme sports?

IF LISA HAD A THEME SONG IT WOULD BE

"I'm the Greatest Star"

LISA NICOLE CARSON

"I've been knocked around a little bit—but I'm still standing."
Nicole Carson, discussing her roller-coaster first season on Ally McBeal with ET Online

Lisa Nicole's star sign suits her—and Renee Radick—to a tee. A cancer (rumor has it she has a crab tattoo on her stomach) she's nurturing and supportive (a good thing in a best friend/roommate/slumber party date), emotional (explains spontaneous blues singing and tendency to beat the poop out of mashers), and well, occasionally crabby (see: tendency to beat the poop out of mashers).

Lisa's chart shows her vitality, great love of music, steamy sexuality, an intense desire for attention and success and, oh yeah, one mean competitive streak.

Lisa Nicole Carson
Born: July 20, 1970
Brooklyn, New York
Sign: Cancer

Now that showboating, relationship-wrecking soul duet with Dr. Greg Butters makes sense.

"Strong and independent? Yes. Sassy? Bite your tongue."
—Entertainment Weekly

61

McSnippets...
What's in Ally's Fridge

Low-fat mineral water, Jell-O, Pringles, tubes of contraceptive jelly (look, I told you: It's love's lottery ticket), a six-pack of Sam Adams, homemade pecan pie, a doggy bag of pasta puttanesca from date night before, Gatorade, Powerbars (keeps 'em chewy), sun-dried tomatoes, imported black olives, fresh lox, asparagus, Ben & Jerry's Heath Bar Crunch ice cream, Omaha steaks, a lime for doing body shots when the whole firm comes to visit ...What? It's almost completely empty? Oh. I guess I haven't actually gone shopping in the past six months, except for that can of Pringles ...

DOROTHY HANDELMAN

McSnippets...

What's In Ally's Briefcase

Notes from morning meeting with Fish on favorite yellow legal pad ... it's funny how the mind wanders, isn't it? Underneath, on yesterday's favorite legal pad, with notes from yesterday's meeting with Fish: possible theme songs. Selections include, "You Don't Own Me" (under-lined), "Stand By Your Man" (crossed out sixteen times), "I Am Woman" (hanging-woman doodle next to it). Hidden in back flap: prescription-only ultra-mega-strength canister of Binaca and last year's special horoscope issue of *Self*, which said that Scorpios would be reuniting with past loves. Mirror to check for lipstick on teeth (but what did I do with the cap of the lipstick ...) and hidden underneath, a faded photograph of Billy and Renee at the 1994 Head of the Charles boat race. My copy of *The Rules*. (You never know.) Some emergency contraceptive jelly and K-Y, in case I ever get caught in the conference room with Bil—I mean, some client. (It is love's lottery ticket, after all.) Blockbuster card, for those exciting nights out on the town. A WE card for Women's Empowerment that I got in the mail, which offers special discounts at car rental agencies and certain hotels. I should get *something* out of my gender but grief, for God's sake.

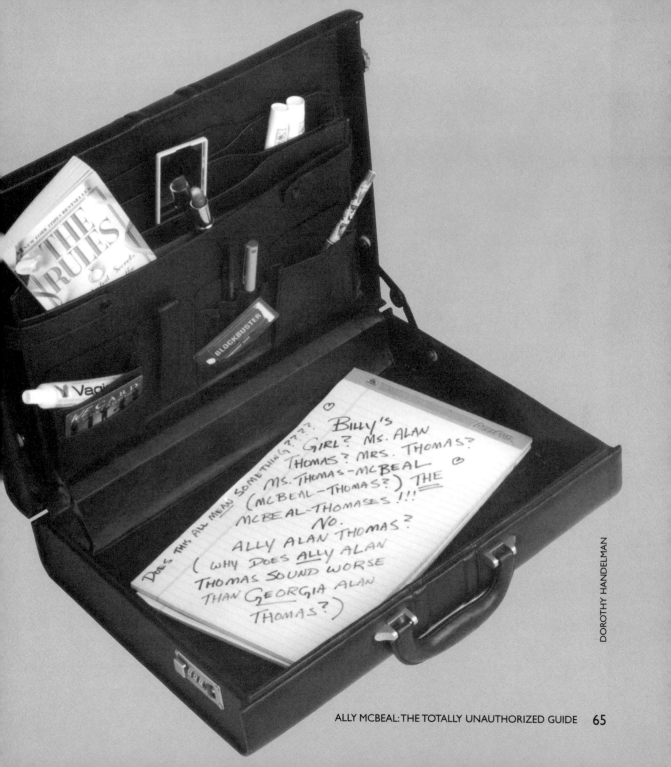

DOROTHY HANDELMAN

McSnippets...
Ally's McBooks
Poke into some of the tomes in Ally's library:

bridget jones's diary — helen fielding — VIKING

THE COMPLETE POEMS ANNE SEXTON

VINTAGE — CARVER — WHAT WE TALK ABOUT WHEN WE TALK ABOUT LOVE

Persuasion — Jane Austen

Ariel — SYLVIA PLATH

Sophie Hannah

An Unsuitable Attachment — Barbara Pym — PYM

No Fond Return of Love — Barbara Pym

Other One **(when in doubt, turn to** ette), *By Myself* **(birthday gift from** ee), *Bridget Jones's Diary* **(I didn't** te *at all . . . I mean, I don't smoke,* k, or worry about my weight, and a virgin . . . or I might as well be), at We Talk About When We Talk About Love **(God, that Raymond Carver guy really knew what he was talking about! These people are even more depressed than I am!),** *Fear of Flying* **(bought copy during college in my women's studies phase),** *An Unsuitable Attachment* **and** *No Fond Return of Love* **(do I like Barbara Pym? I haven't read them yet . . . something about the**

titles just spoke to me), *Common Law and Common Sense* **(gotta have something for weekends at the Cape, and I should brush up on both),** *The Rules* **(I think I left this in my briefcase . . .), all my old Judy Blume books from junior high (I still always really relate to all the narrators),** *Persuasion* **(worked hard to find copy without the movie tie-in cover),** *Ariel* **and** *The Colossus* **(God, that Sylvia Plath chick could be scary! What was she so worried about? I mean, she had Ted Hughes, after all . . .),** *The Complete Poems of Anne Sexton* **(this Sexton chick makes Sylvia Plath and Raymond Carver look like Georgia and Bil—I mean, the Dancing Twins . . .)**

McSnippets ...
Music-Ally Speaking
I can't listen to Vonda Shepard *all* the time ...

Now I threw these all over my floor when **Baby Cha-cha** tried a sneak attack last night, so I don't know if you can see everything, but there's *Lilith Fair: A Celebration of Women in Music;* **everything by Natalie Merchant, Sara McLachlan, Jewel, Paula Cole, Meredith Brooks, and all the other cute grrls in vintage dresses with guitars (Grrl Power!);** *The Fifth Dimension: Greatest Hits of All Time* **(for singing the "Wedding Bell Blues"); some old Go-Go's albums from high school; a James Taylor box set (for singing the plain ol' white girl blues);** *I Do Not Want What I Haven't Got* **(I put "Nothing Compares to U" on repeat play when I'm feeling low about Billy);** *The Immaculate Collection* **(dancer-ific Madonna hits perfect for slumber parties with Renee);** *Johnny Mathis: Greatest Hits* **(he's perfect for impromptu slow dances at office);** *Carole King: Tapestry* **(I sang "It's Too Late" in seventh-grade talent show), some Diana Ross (God—look how fat she used to be!), some Gladys Knight and the Pips (I'm practicing), Carly Simon's** *Boys in the Trees* **(I always cry thinking of her and James's breakup, too), for bad moods,** *Garbage* **(I really relate to the lyric "I only like it when its complicated"), and my old records from** *Grease* **and** *Cinderella* **(oh, shut up! You kept them, too!).**

McSnippets...
What's in Ally's Medicine Chest

You know, the usual ... Ponds blackhead removal pads (they don't actually do anything, but ripping them off *feels* so good), tubes of contraceptive jelly (it's love's lottery ticket, okay? And I don't know how much I spend on it a month!), ancient, fuzz-covered bottle of Enjoli perfume bought in high school (for nostalgia, and because the "I'm a Woman" jingle makes a good theme song), Gyne-Lotrimin 3 (I'm so psyched they got the three-day treatment! If only I could get my hands on some of that one-day stuff! Maybe Renee could get me some from her off days, when she appears on *ER* ...), Vaginal Contraceptive Film (this stuff looked cool...and you never know ...), baby powder (for after all those long walks in high heels), and lots and lots of contraceptive Jell-O—I mean *jelly* (it works like Kryptonite on that stupid dancing baby).

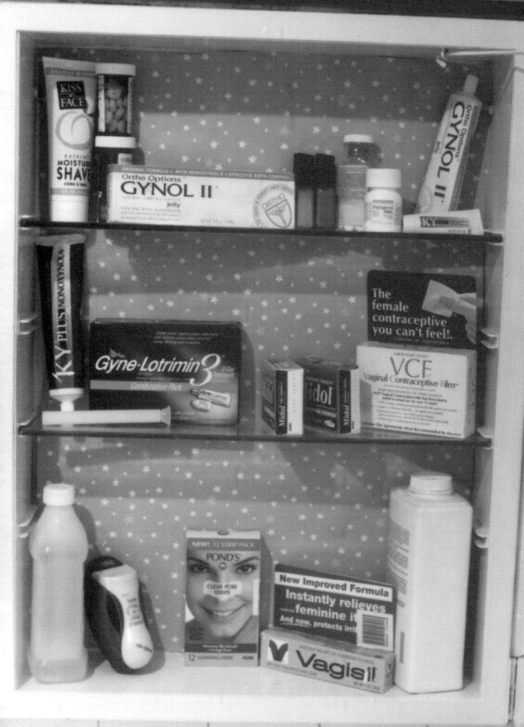

THE TOP TEN
REASONS ...
WE

1. SHE'S FASHION FORWARD

"Whenever I get depressed, I raise my hemlines.
If things don't change, I'm bound to get arrested."

2. SHE'S A FEARLESS FIGHTER FOR GENDER EQUITY

"Where does it say that women can't act like men sometimes? I saw a piece of cute
meat, and I said to myself, 'You only live once: Be a man.' "

3. SHE DOESN'T NEED A MAN TO MAKE HERSELF MISERABLE

"It doesn't matter that I'm not in a relationship with anybody. Sometimes I feel
like I'm being unfaithful to myself."

4. SHE'S AN OPTIMIST

"Today is going to be a less bad day. I can feel it. Sometimes I wake up and
I just know that everything is going to be . . . less bad."

5. SHE BELIEVES ANITA HILL

"Why can't he be a man and just paw me a little? I am a sexual object,
for God's sake. What, he couldn't give me a little grope?"

LOVE ALLY

6. SHE'S MODEST TO A FAULT

"I know I've got it great—really good job, good friends, good family, total freedom, and long bubble baths. What else could there be?"

7. SHE'S A PACIFIST

(After tripping a woman in that infamous supermarket scuffle over a can of Pringles): "I didn't mean for her to fall; I only meant for her to stumble."

8. SHE'S ECUMENICAL

"I never dated a rabbi before. I hope he's funnier than the priest."

9. SHE SUPPORTS FAMILY VALUES

"I have to believe that it works. Love, couplehood, partnerships—the idea that when people come together, they stay together. I have to take that with me to bed, even if I have to go to bed alone."

10. SHE'S ALWAYS GOT A JOB AT HALLMARK IF THE LAWYER THING DOESN'T WORK OUT

"Love and law are the same, romantic in concept—but the actual practice can get you a yeast infection."

Bringing Up Ally

How did Ally get to be Ally? Well, we don't exactly know, and in case you haven't noticed, Ally spends an hour every Monday night trying to answer the same question. In fact, David Kelley hasn't revealed all that much about his character beyond the fact that she majored in art history as an undergraduate and attended Harvard Law School. We know Ally has a "loving" family, because she's said so herself, but then, she managed only one long-distance phone call to her parents in an entire year, and her father has appeared only in a couple of flashback cameos. So Ally's family life and childhood remain a mystery. The only thing we know for sure is that she's been on-again, off-again with Billy since she was seven years old.

Of course, we do know a little bit about the era Ally grew up in—and can make some pretty good guesses about her youth by looking at the captivating, if befuddled, grown-up character she is today. Not that we can get too *specific*—we'd look awfully silly saying Ally had two sisters only to find out next season that she was an only child. But we're probably not going too far out on a limb by saying that hers was a typical American girlhood in the Madonna era, that she grew up in comfortable middle-class surroundings, and that even back when she was cruising the mall in Esprit sweatshirt wear, Ally was something of a dreamer. Use this time line to fill in, at least partially, some of the rest of her developmental blanks:

April 6, 1970, Someplace, USA: Ally McBaby is born. Or so we think—since this is also the date of the airing of her 28th birthday party episode, "Happy Birthday Baby."

1971: Hot pants become a fad, making lasting impression on leg consciousness of baby Ally.

1972: Olga Korbut, "the elf from Grodno," single-handedly changes gymnastics into a teeny woman's sport by winning gold in 1976. (In 1997, Ally McBeal single-handedly changes lawyering into a teeny woman's sport).

1973: Develops lifelong passion for justice watching Lynda Carter fight crime, defend American Way, and squeeze self into red, white and blue girdle as Wonder Woman.

1974: Blue Suede charges up the charts with cheesy ballad "Hooked on a Feeling," making lasting impression on still blissfully Baby Huggy-free Ally McBeal. Also, girls are allowed to play Little League for first time.

1975: Tabei Junko becomes first woman to scale Mount Everest. Five-year-old Ally does the Hustle in celebration.

1976: Jodie Foster stars in *Taxi Driver*. Six-year-old Ally learns the power of showing off lots of leg while wearing big, chunky heels.

1977: Ally McBeal meets Billy Allen Thomas for first time. Also experiences first Ally-style fantasy, picturing self as Princess Leia, ballet teacher as Darth Vader.

1978: Sees *Grease*; begins to have grown-up feelings of hopeless devotion toward Billy—and grease monkey John Travolta.

1979: Ally demands figure-skating outfit—and Seeing Eye dog—for birthday in an effort to mimic the tragic heroine of her favorite movie, *Ice Castles*.

1980: EEOC bans sexual harassment of employees by their supervisors. Too bad Ally's butt-squeezing future boss, Jack Billings, wasn't paying attention . . .

1981: Fifth-grade Ally, consumed by massive Rick Springfield crush, vows to one day become *Jesse's Girl*.

1982: Are you there, God? It's me, Ally. Pre-pubescent McBeal exiles *Misty of Chincoteague* from bookcase to make room for the complete works of Judy Blume.

1983: Gives up charge account at unicorn sticker store, acquires expression "for sure" to match aquamarine sweatshirt dress, decides she likes Cyndi Lauper more than Madonna.

1984: Dislocates shoulder trying to squeeze gel out of tube to style new asymmetrical haircut.

1985: Sees *The Breakfast Club* fifteen times with boyfriend Billy. Replaces *Sixteen Candles* as favorite movie until *Pretty in Pink* comes out the next year.

1986: Cast as "Day-by-Day" girl in school production of *Godspell*; demoted to tech crew after turning rehearsal into forum on separation of church and state.

1987: Sprains ankle dancing with Billy at junior prom attempting to "bust a move" during Paula Abdul dance remix.

1988: Graduates from high school, sense of cool forever scarred by being elected "girl

The thirteen-going-on-thirty star of Taxi Driver . . .

most likely to become Julie Andrews." Experiences recurring vision of self in dirndl, sewing rompers out of ugly green drapes ...

1989: Collegiate Ally trades in makeup for book of Anne Sexton poems and highlighter. Decides shaving legs, regular showers and all scents but Patchouli are tools of phallocentric oppression.

1990: Flirts with bisexuality after attending a Sweet Honey in the Rock South Africa benefit concert at student center.

1991: By day, intern at National Organization for Women. By night, guilt-ridden fan of *Beverly Hills 90210*.

1992: With roommates, makes huge sacrificial bonfire of copies of *What Color Is Your Parachute?* graduation-gift books.

1993: Begins paper chase by following Billy to Harvard Law School; also cramming by the Charles are Renee Radick and Richard Fish.

1994: Ally makes *Law Review*—go Crimson! Billy doesn't, and the sour grapes transfers to the University of Michigan—go Wolverines!

1995: Insert your own postcollegiate, on-again, off-again, long-distance, fear-of-commitment, messy breakup relationship here. Change names to "Ally" and "Billy." Voilà!

1996: Ally and Renee cross the river to become fabulous, sexy, incredibly un-Boston Boston lawyers.

1997: Harassed by law partner Jack Billings; offered new job at Cage/Fish; discovers Billy also works there. And is married ...

... and the blindly triumphant heroine of Ice Castles

Love Means Always Having to Say You're Sorry

The admissions committee apparently never guessed the ugly truth: Ally's decision to attend Harvard Law School was largely motivated by a desire to be near Billy—giver of her first kiss, the man who she lost her innocence to, and the man she planned on marrying—not to become the next Ruth Bader Ginsberg. Later she discovered that law was an equal passion. But in the process, the love of these two childhood sweethearts went blooey all over Harvard Square.

Only two ridiculously overcompetitive yuppies would end a relationship over who made the *Law Review* and who didn't. So it's not surprising that when Ally was asked to join the staff of the prestigious journal and Billy wasn't, things went south . . . actually, midwest. It seems being shown up by his girlfriend was more than Billy could take. He left Harvard (and Ally) for the University of Michigan (and met his *Michigan Law Review* editor, Georgia).

This sad story has a wrinkle you may be unaware of. It seems there's a strong possibility that Ally and Billy's love wasn't merely done in by academic bickering and pride. It could be their love was done in by . . . Harvard.

Let this be a warning to all young couples—there may be relationship poison in that famous Ivy. Indeed, Billy and Ally aren't the most famous pair whose union was doomed by a Crimson connection. That honor goes to trust-fund baby Oliver Barrett IV and plucky scholarship girl Jenny Cavilleri, whose treacly *Love Story* had a far grimmer ending. Okay, so Ally didn't get a terminal disease; she was terminally heartbroken by the breakup. And the comparisons between Ally's story and that other story don't end there . . .

LOVE STORY

CENTRAL CHARACTER:
Sassy gal in miniskirts played by Ali McGraw

LOVE INTEREST:
Serious, uptight young lawyer named Barrett

INITIAL HURDLE:
Disapproving parents say she's from the wrong side of the tracks

KEY ROMANTIC MOMENT:
Couple rebels against convention and decide to get married

HEROINE'S ANNOYING TIC:
Has annoying habit of calling lover "Preppy"

ROMANCE DOOMED BY:
Jenny's terminal case of cancer

POPPYCOCK DISGUISED AS HOMESPUN WISDOM:
Ali thinks love means never having to say you're sorry

ALLY'S STORY

CENTRAL CHARACTER:
Sassy gal in miniskirts named Ally McBeal

LOVE INTEREST:
Serious, uptight young lawyer named Billy

INITIAL HURDLE:
Disapproving friends think psychologically "jumped the track"

KEY ROMANTIC MOMENT:
Couple rebels against convention and decides to flirt while he's married

HEROINE'S ANNOYING TIC:
She has this annoying habit of *calling*

ROMANCE DOOMED BY:
Terminal case of Georgia

POPPYCOCK DISGUISED AS HOMESPUN WISDOM:
Ally thinks love causes yeast infections

Desira-Billy-ty

Billy. Ally's oldest, dearest friend, true love and soul mate. Who went and married some tart from *Melrose Place*. As Ally's therapist Dr. Tracey Clark (and nearly everyone else who watches the show) knows, Ally's got to permanently delete him from her Good Boyfriend Material database. Too bad she can't. This is the guy she played doctor with as a tot. The is the guy who used to make her sleep next to an open phone line, so that even when he wasn't there, he could hear her breathing as she slept. This is the guy who works down the hall. And he's a nice, supportive, caring guy at that.

Sure, Billy *says* he's devastatingly happily married to the annoyingly gorgeous, gratingly competent Georgia. But for a happy hubby, he seems awfully happy to offer Ally a shoulder to cry on when she gets wobbly . . . about every five minutes. And Billy's still possessive and jealous when Ally goes out with other men. Georgia already knows what Billy pretends not to—he's still in love with his grade school honey.

Not that they're an obvious couple, even if Billy wasn't shacked up with Malibu Barbie. Unlike the other Froot Loops at Cage/Fish & Associates, Billy takes the law very seriously. An ambitious attorney who made *Michigan Law Review* and clerked for a Supreme Court Justice, deep in his heart, Billy obviously has a fetish for nut jobs the way his school chum Richard digs neck wattles. What's more, under that choirboy smile he has a sleazy side: the no-account dog who would sleep with a hooker at his bachelor party. Sure, Ally made Bill feel bad about it, but *really*. But maybe it's that mixture of saint and scoundrel that drives women nutty (it certainly isn't that weird, off-kilter Caesar haircut he sported for a while). Exactly one-half of all the women in Allyworld are head over heels for him.

It's certainly a lucky fellow who gets to be the love object of both Courtney Thorne-Smith and Calista Flockhart, but easygoing actor Gil Bellows seems to take it in stride.

> "*I'm the Harvey Korman of the show. I'm the one who's laughing at what everyone else is doing.*"
> —Gil Bellows at a Directors' Guild discussion of Ally McBeal

GIL BELLOWS

TAKE OFF, YOUR HOSER!

Like Alan Thicke, Sour Patch Kids, and Quebec separatism, Gil Bellows is Canadian. He was born and raised in Vancouver, British Columbia, but headed south to attend the American Academy of Dramatic Arts in southern California. He has appeared onstage in California and New York.

IS THE NAME "GIL" REALLY CANADIAN FOR "HIT ME"?

Yes, unless you are a really good-looking and successful TV star. Some cool Gils: Gil Gerard, who dared to wear spandex as TV's Buck Rogers; Gil-gamesh, Mesopotamian hero who starred in his very own epic back in the third century BC; feminist scholar Carol Gil-ligan; and Gil-bert O'Sullivan, supremely cheesy 1970s pop star who sang "Alone Again, Naturally," featured on an *Ally* episode of the same name.

SORRY, GIRLS, BUT HE'S NEVER *HOME ALONE*

Bellows is married to the depressingly radiant Rya Kihlstedt, an actress who made the mistake of playing psychotoddler fodder in *Home Alone 3*. Note to Rya: Fire your agent.

MUST-FLEE TV

Pre-*Ally*, Gil acted with two of NBC's "Women of Monday Night"—Kristie Alley (in the TV movie *Radiant City*) and Tea Leoni (as a guest star in her short-lived series *Flying Blind*). In *Silver Strand* he played a Navy Seal opposite *Knots Landing* hussy Nicollette Sheridan (darn! no *Nicollette's Closet* ... yet!) and first came to court in a small shot on *Law & Order*.

YOU CALL THIS A PRISON MOVIE? WITHOUT LINDA BLAIR?

Bellows's breakout role was a supporting part as an inmate in the studiously uplifting but way, way, way too long jailhouse tale, *The Shawshank Redemption*.

Y'ALL DON'T COME BACK NOW, Y'HEAR?

In *Love and a .45*, a serial killin' hillbilly flick in the mode of *Natural Born Killers*, Gil starred as Watty Watts, a murdering fugitive gunnin' for Mexico with his cracker moll Starlene—also known as Renee Zellweger.

MIAMI MCBEAL

Before he was the hapless ex-boyfriend of dizzy romantic Ally McBeal, Bellows was the hapless fiancee of dizzy romantic Sarah Jessica Parker in the 1995 Woody-Allen-gets-a-sex-change-and-moves-to-Florida comedy *Miami Rhapsody*. The next year he appeared with Parker in the New York publishing drama *The Substance of Fire*.

THRONG TO THE BAR, CRYING ALL, "GUILTY! GUILTY!"

Bellows had a small role in Al Pacino's tribute to Shakespeare, *Looking for Richard*. Other films Gil has recently

acted in are: *Dinner at Fred's* with Parker Posey, *The Assistant* with Joan Plowright, and *The Judas Kiss* with Emma Thompson.

IF GIL HAD A THEME SONG IT WOULD BE ...
The theme song from *Gil-ligan's Island*

Billy on the other side of the law: Gil Bellows stars as a hard-edged convict in The Shawshank Redemption

The Ex-Files

Here's what really sucks about Ally's breakup with Billy: Even though they officially broke it off years ago, he's still around. How's Ally supposed to get on with her life, meet and settle down with a guy like Richard Cheanie or Dr. Greg Butters—and be satisfied that he's an adequate replacement—when the guy she wants to replace doesn't have the good manners to trip into the office shredder? As long as Billy's around being "supportive," getting all moony eyed whenever Ally does something quintessentially Ally and periodically declaring that he still has some of those old coals burning for her (always conveniently

Ally with yummy model . . .

when she's found somebody new), she's in love limbo. There's no hope for her unless Billy moves, dies, or loses the rest of his hair and grows a Sam Adams paunch.

So now that we've decided Ally must kill Billy, how she should do it and not get caught (reminder: kill Elaine first to plug any possible leaks). Oh, lighten up. *Teasing.*

You have to admit, though, that back in the day when *ex* usually meant *exterminated* these messy emotional loose ends were easier to tie up. It's not like Henry VIII got all *freaked out* every time he saw Ann Boleyn walk by

his cubicle. After all, it was over, she was over. He was happily chewing on a mutton chop with a lady-in-waiting; Ann's head was rolling around in a bucket—bygones.

Over the centuries we've gotten progres-

sively less able to dispatch unwanted ex-lovers in an efficient way, until we've reached the wishy-washy Ally-Billy era. They could take some pointers from these notable pairs of exes:

. . . *and buttery doctor*

Will Ally choose or lose Cheanie?

EVERETT COLLECTION: © 20TH-CENTURY FOX

Dumper: Aeneas
Dumpee: Dido of Carthage
Reasons for Breakup:
Clingy Carthaginian wants to settle down, live life of middle-brow North African desperation, disapproves of career goal of founding Rome
Breakup Technique:
Says going out for six-pack, sails for Italy instead
Fate of Dumpee:
Wakes up banging pots and pans, tosses self from balcony
Postbreakup Baggage:
Custody battle involving Mediterranean resolved by reducing Carthage to rubble and sowing ground with salt

Dumper: Nora, from Ibsen's "A Doll's House"
Dumpee: Torvald, still in the doghouse
Reasons for Breakup: Chauvinist hubby stifles demands for gender equity
Breakup Technique: Compares suffocating bourgeois life to being Tickle Me Inga
Fate of Dumpee: Forced to eat Stouffer's Lutefisk and Lingonberry microwave dinners
Postbreakup Baggage: Ryvita crumbs in bed

Dumper: Frankie
Dumpee: Johnny
Reasons for Breakup: Was her man, but he done her wrong
Breakup Technique: .44 revolver
Fate of Dumpee: Done gone
Postbreakup Baggage: Joins support group in order to get over feelings there "ain't no good in men"

Dumper: Liz
Dumpee: Dick
Reasons for Breakup: Acid-tongued Welsh freeloader said no such thing as "violet" eyes, had irrational fear of Virginia Woolf

Fate of Dumpee: Drowns self, career, in cocktails and painkillers
Postbreakup Baggage: Is checked in at Betty Ford

Dumper: Donald
Dumpee: Ivana
Reasons for Breakup: Bodysnatched by a Gabor sister
Breakup Technique: Sent hag one-way to Mar-a-Largo on Czech bus lines
Fate of Dumpee: Forced to peddle Chanel knockoffs to trailer trash
Postbreakup Baggage: Daughter whose name is mallard mating call

Dumper: Andrew, Duke of York
Dumpee: Sarah Ferguson
Reasons for Breakup: Spendthrift commoner took frivolous weekends in Gstaad, allowed American to suck toes
Breakup Technique: Went home to mum
Fate of Dumpee: Forced to peddle food knockoffs to trailer trash
Postbreakup Baggage: Princess Anne's softball team

down one equipment manager
Dumper: Pamela Anderson Lee
Dumpee: Tommy Lee
Reasons for Breakup: Loutish behavior means he's Crue-sing for a bruising
Breakup Technique: Deadly weapon Gloria Allred
Fate of Dumpee: Instead of picking guitar with teeth, picking trash up with pole
Postbreakup Baggage: Taped over it with funny *Barbed Wire* outtakes

Dumper: Warsaw Pact
Dumpee: Russia
Reasons for Breakup: Couldn't stop Mother Russia-ing, squandered hard-earned savings trying to keep up with Reagans
Breakup Technique: Started seeing other people in Western Europe
Fate of Dumpee: Series of nervous breakdowns, hit vodka hard, stopped going to gym
Postbreakup Baggage: At least baggage no longer handled by Aeroflot

Georgia on Our Minds

Georgia's talented, beautiful, sweet, successful, levelheaded and married to a nice guy. In high school, she probably was homecoming queen, president of the Glee Club and student body VP.

In short, she's Ally's worst nightmare.

But the worst thing about Georgia is that she's genuinely nice—the kind of gal who apologizes in the middle of a kick-boxing match (she and Ally squared off in a tension-loosening bout . . . and knocked each other out). She genuinely likes Ally—though she doesn't like her drooling all over her husband—and they have built an uneasy friendship. But even though she seems perfect, this Valkyrie has her problems: Like Ally, she came to Cage/Fish after a sexual harassment suit—her old boss transferred her out of the litigation department because his wife thought she was too attractive. Worse, the poor thing has developed a huge complex about being compared to a Barbie doll. Hate to be frank, but swell as she is, Georgia wouldn't look entirely out of place in her own pink plastic dream house.

Thankless role? Courtney-Thorne Smith denies it. In interviews, she's keen to say how much she L!-O!-V!-E! *loves* Calista. But then, playing the straight woman against a hallucinating nymph is a step up from getting stabbed in the back every week by Heather Locklear . . .

SEARCHIN' THE TRASH TONIGHT

Courtney was born on November 8, 1968 (um, the Autumn of Love?), in San Francisco. She grew up in mellow Mill Valley, California. Her totally organic parents oppressed her by banning sugared cereal from the house. Once her mother bought a box of Lucky Charms, but regretted it and threw them away. Junk-food-starved Courtney then spent a week rummaging through the garbage to dig out handfuls. And yet nobody called Child Welfare.

GIDGET GOES TO HOLLYWOOD

After acting briefly with the Mill Valley Players in her hometown, Courtney hit the surf, playing sunny California blondes in hard-hitting films such as Welcome to 18, Summer School, (with future Chicago Hope doc Mark Hamill),

> *"Get your paws off my husband."*
>
> —Courtney Thorne-Smith on what unexpressed thoughts might lurk behind Georgia's sunny smile, in TV Guide

COURTNEY THORNE-SMITH

and *Revenge of the Nerds II: Nerds in Paradise*, in which she played a character named Sunny. In 1986, she played sunny California blonde Stacy Hamilton on the sitcom *Fast Times at Ridgemont High*.

WHAT'S THE DEFINITION OF "WILLOWY"?
(a) Graceful, tall and slender.
(b) Adjective used to describe all characters played by Courtney Thorne-Smith.

WE USUALLY THROW IN THE EXTRA COREY FOR FREE . . .
Courtney played another teen beauty in the critically acclaimed coming-of-age story *Lucas*, which also starred the thinner half of the "two Coreys," Corey Haim, and Charlie "scandal-Velcro" Sheen. It also introduced the world to a whippersnapper named Winona Ryder.

GIMME A C (II)
In a career stretch, Courtney moved away from playing high school cheer-leader types to tackle the recurring role of a professional cheerleader on *L.A. Law*. As Kimberly the Laker Girl, she got her first taste of David Kelley-craft-ed courtroom hijinks. After that role, she put down her pom-poms to play a (surprise!) girl-next-door type on the sitcom *Day by Day* with another future selfish Elaine—Elaine Benes, that is—Julia Louis-Dreyfus.

COINCIDENCE? YOU BE THE JUDGE
For five years on steamy *Melrose Place*, Courtney played the show's moral center—incest-surviving alcoholic Allison Parker Hanson. Sometimes she got called Ally, and the love of her life happened to be named . . . Billy.

WATCH YOUR BACK, ALLY
She may look sugar-and-spice, but while still lounging by the *Melrose* pool, Courtney filmed the trashy-cool TV movie *Beauty's Revenge*, about a Midwestern beauty queen who goes on a murder spree when her man strays.

WELL, AT LEAST HIS NAME'S NOT GIL
Courtney capitalized on the success of *Ally McBeal* by starring in the upcom-ing movie *Chairman of the Board* with hunky sensation Matt Damon. Whoops, we meant hunky sensation . . . Carrot Top.

IF COURTNEY HAD A THEME SONG, IT WOULD BE . . .
"Barbie Girl"

Courtney in the short-lived TV series, Fast Times at Ridgemont High

The stars say Courtney's a person who would allow her hubby to take risks in a relationship, though it's unclear if regularly hugging his ex-girlfriend would be one of them. How's this for unholy astrological coincidences—both Billy's women are Scorpios!

Courtney's star chart reveals that underneath her air of confidence is an emotionally complex and sensitive type, with an ability to see both sides of an issue (aha—perhaps that explains the friendship with the other woman).

Courtney Thorne-Smith
Born: November 8, 1968
San Francisco, California
Sign: Scorpio

But what truly defines Courtney is a cheerful, gung-ho attitude toward life, perfect for someone who's made a career of playing pom-pom girls and perky girls-next-door.

On the flip side, fidelity is supposed to be very important to this Scorpian, so an unfaithful beau might feel her sting.

93

McMelrose Place

There's a good reason why Georgia seems relatively unperturbed by the fact that her husband regularly flirts with a beautiful ex-lover at the office. She's been through it all before—or at least Courtney Thorne-Smith has. And at least in this case, she's relatively sure that Ally's not going to fake a pregnancy, show up in a sexy negligee at the beach house or cut the brake lines in her car.

All and all, Cage/Fish & Associates is a far less hostile environment than her old workplace, D&D Advertising . . . although the dress code is pretty much the same. When it comes to short skirts, smoldering old flames, office gossip and catfights, Courtney's new colleagues are prime-time amateur hour:

ALLY MCBEAL	MELROSE PLACE
Boss is money-hungry blond named Richard Fish, cracks "Fishisms"	**Boss** is money-hungry blonde named Amanda Woodward, refines art of Bitchism
Ally loves Billy, pretends she's over him	**Ally** loves Billy, pretends she's blind to wreck marriage
Law firm office is improbably cushy place—colleagues meet frequently in Unisex	**Ad agency** office is improbably cushy place—colleagues meet frequently to have sex in bathroom, offices, cars, parking garages, elevator, pool, beach house, Kinko's …
Ally is forced to tell dirty joke at favorite bar, apparently the only one in town	**Ally** is forced to play dirty pool at favorite bar, Shooter's, apparently the only one in town
Nosy assistant Elaine snoops in Ally's business, triggering events that lead to bar review panel on her emotional stability	**Nosy assistant** Brooke snoops through Amanda's files, discovers abandoned husband, which leads to murder, affair with would-be hit man, and another murder
Beautiful and brilliant career woman Ally is prone to vivid daydreams urging her to act on amorous feelings for her true love, Billy, or at least to tell him how she feels	**Beautiful and brilliant** career woman Kimberly is prone to vivid daydreams urging her to act on murderous feelings for true love Michael, or at least to give him lobotomy
Kooky Ally reunites with true love, only to find he's married to someone else	**Kooky Sydney** reunites with true love, only to be mowed down by speeding car on her wedding day

Back Allys

After just a year Ally's had enough bad first dates, kooky fantasies and cringe-inducing embarrassing moments to build her therapist a retirement villa in Boca. Episode after episode introduced eccentric characters and kinky plot lines and led us deeper into Ally's maze of mixed-up emotions. Sure, she could be neurotic and flighty, but she also could be both compassionate and tough. Yes, tough. Whatever her self-doubts and slipups, Ally does seem to be growing both as a lawyer and as a human being.

But let's hope that next season she doesn't evolve into some dull, day-dream-free, 100-percent-Bar-Association-approved emotionally stable type. What was terrific about Ally's first season was her maddeningly two-steps-forward, two-steps-back pursuit of her dreams. Occasionally, Ally fell flat on her face. But in the end we always wound up rooting for her (and prayed she would spend summer vacation learning how to walk in high heels). Which brings us to this sassy celebration of Ally's first year of incredibly trippy Monday nights:

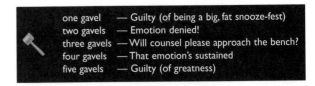

one gavel — Guilty (of being a big, fat snooze-fest)
two gavels — Emotion denied!
three gavels — Will counsel please approach the bench?
four gavels — That emotion's sustained
five gavels — Guilty (of greatness)

ALLY MCBEAL PILOT
Original Airdate: September 8, 1997

This flashback-heavy premiere introduces us to the divine Ms. M. We learn why she initially went to Harvard (where she was more interested in a Mrs. than a J.D.), watch her sue sleazebag butt-grabbing boss Jack Billings for sexual harassment and meet all the quirky denizens of Allyworld.

COMMENTARY

Minus Cage, that is. Sadly, this first episode is Biscuit-free. But we do get something unheard of in a lawyer show. Ally takes on a cakewalk censorship case . . . and loses. (Okay, she goes on to win on appeal, but it's a start.) Remember: Sexual harassment is bad for lawyers and other living things. Watch this in reruns and share your worst workplace war stories with friends. Burn candles. Burn sacrificial effigies. Just don't burn this.

VERDICT

MCTRIVIA

In the pilot Jack Billings (actor Richard Riehle) claims he pinches behinds because he has obsessive-compulsive disorder. Which of the following is *not* a common symptom of obsessive-compulsive disorder?

a. Excessive hand washing
b. Extreme slowness
c. Always arriving early
d. Repetitive task checking

Answer: b

2 "COMPROMISING POSITIONS"
Original Airdate: September 15, 1997

The Biscuit shows up. He's been arrested for soliciting a prostitute, and Ally discovers Billy and creepy tooth-lovin' Judge Happy Boyle both shagged a call girl at Billy's stag night.

COMMENTARY

First of many Ally Mc-Hooker shows, in which characters vastly oversimplify the difference between male and female views of sex and love. At least on Kelley's show, however, he's an equal-opportunity employer: instead of relegating hooker roles to only females, throughout the season his tricks are both boys and girls. Resolved: Women are from Venus, men are from Ur ... well, you know.

VERDICT

 *This episode is Ally Gold. Not least because it marks the first appearance of brazen hussy Whipper Cone.*

MCTRIVIA

In "Compromising Positions" we are introduced to Ally's first non-Billy love interest, rich client Ronald Cheanie (Tate Donovan). Before his abortive on-screen love affair with Ally, Donovan had abortive off-screen love affairs with:

a. Julia Roberts and Daphne Zuniga
b. Sandra Bullock and Jennifer Aniston
c. Jenna Elfman and Marisa Tomei
d. The Barbie Twins

Answer: b

3 "THE KISS"
Original Airdate: September 22, 1997

On their first date new client Ronald Cheanie just pecks Ally on the cheek. *Big* mistake. In a subplot Ally and Georgia represent fired newscaster Barbara Cooker (ex-Charlie's Angel Kate Jackson) in an age discrimination suit. Opposing counsel turns out to be none other than bilious Jack Billings.

COMMENTARY

NOW-friendly part of episode: Georgia and Ally join forces to fight sexism—and win. Cringe-worthy backlash part: Victory makes them fret they'll wind up like lonely dried-up old single hags like Cooker—even though "hag" Kate Jackson actually looks smashing. With pushing-AARP-age babes like Susan Sarandon, Gloria Steinem, Felicia Rashad and Diane Keaton running around, isn't it time to retire that old no-life-after-50 routine?

VERDICT

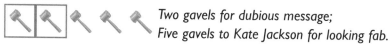

Two gavels for dubious message;
Five gavels to Kate Jackson for looking fab.

MCTRIVIA

Before Charlie signed them up as Angels, actresses Kate Jackson and Cheryl Ladd both:

a. Tried out for Beelzebub's pep squad in *Satan's School for Girls*
b. Secured overhead compartments as stewardess trainees with Connie Sellecca on the show *Flying High*
c. Lost out to Cybill Shepard for the part of a small town beauty queen in *The Last Picture Show*
d. Dated diminutive pop singer Paul Williams

Answer: a

4 "THE AFFAIR"
Original Airdate: September 22, 1998

Ally's former law professor, Jack Dawson, croaks, and his widow asks her to speak at the funeral. Only thing is, Ally had an affair with the guy. Meanwhile Elaine introduces the world to the face bra.

COMMENTARY

An instant classic, this episode is made even better because it bids good-bye to drippy, moralizing peck-kisser Ronald Cheanie, who can't take Ally's nuttiness. Good riddance: We couldn't take his wimpiness. As a result of Ally's immediately agreeing to speak at the funeral, hilarious complications ensue, culminating in a typically Ally crash-and-burn eulogy that's terrific.

VERDICT

MCTRIVIA

Kathy Baker, the actress who plays widow Katherine Dawson, is best known as one of the stars of David Kelley's critically acclaimed *Picket Fences*. She received an Academy Award nomination for her work as:

a. A down-and-out drug addict in *Clean and Sober*
b. A down-and-out streetwalker in *Street Smart*
c. A down-on-earth astronaut's wife in *The Right Stuff*
d. A hot-and-bothered Midwesterner in *Edward Scissorhands*

Answer: b

AN "OTHER WOMAN" REFURBISHING RITUAL

It happens to the best of us. You fall for this great, sweet guy, you like him and he likes you, and everything's coming up roses except he's . . . married. Gulp. Where do we go from here? Usually, nowhere fast. But you came out of it older and wiser, if (just a little) sadder, didn't you? This is life with a capital L, but you've seen love from both sides now. And now you know which side you want to be on in the future. So put on the dress you never could wear because he couldn't take you out to dinner in public, the slip you stole from his wife's drawer, and the earrings he gave you for your birthday. (Not a pretty sight, is it?) Then toss them in the Dumpster, pronto. Good girl. Stock up on black coffee and cigarettes.

5 "ONE HUNDRED TEARS AWAY"
Original Airdate: October 20, 1997

A tussle over a can of Pringles leads to Ally assaulting a woman (see, Officer, she trips her, but she doesn't mean for her to actually fall . . .), an arrest for accidentally shoplifting a tube of contraceptive jelly (see, Officer, she put it in her pocket because she was embarrassed . . .) and a bar review panel hearing on her sanity.

COMMENTARY

High marks for the comic scuffle that sends Ally into a downward spiral and Elaine's disastrous testimony to the Bar Association, but Billy's sticky soliloquy about Ally being a free spirit is worse than a bath in cherry cough syrup. Maybe Ally wouldn't have been caught shoplifting contraceptive jelly if that good ol' sponge hadn't been recalled—too bad, like Elaine Benes, she hadn't stocked up. It does seem like an injustice to have to pay for most of the products that guarantee our sexual freedom since, besides leaking, burning, making you gain weight and (sometimes) shooting all over the bathroom, a lot of these babies don't even work. Put your stash on your living room floor and be amazed. Still, it's better than drinking hemlock, isn't it? Kinda.

VERDICT

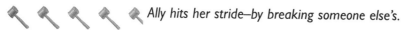 *Ally hits her stride—by breaking someone else's.*

MCTRIVIA

In "One Hundred Tears Away," Elaine "helps" Ally by telling the Bar Association her boss is an unstable woman because she's still in love with her old boyfriend. What woman recently went to trial with an "unstable" defense because of an illegal liaison with a "spiritually old"—but physically pubescent—boyfriend, whom everyone but herself thinks is actually unstable?

a. Mary McFadden
b. Cher
c. Elizabeth Taylor
d. Mary Kay LeTourneau

Answer: d

6 "THE PROMISE"
Original Airdate: October 27, 1997

Ally and Cage defend a high-class call girl who thinks dating is a sham and that selling sex to men is empowering. Meanwhile, Ally advises a hefty fellow lawyer to break off his engagement if he doesn't really love his fiancée, then changes her mind when the fiancée explains hefty people don't have as many options as scrawny little lawyers.

COMMENTARY

Not only are we forced to rehash the tired men-want-sex-women-want-love debate with the prostitute story-line, but will somebody please call the Overweight People's Anti-Defamation League? Who says the large have to settle for less?

VERDICT

 Alert the vice squad already; enough with the hookers.

MCTRIVIA

Redheaded stunner Jamie Rose plays hooker Sandra Winchell in this episode. In the 1980s she played the slutty ingenue on what evening soap?

a. *The Colbys*
b. *Falcon Crest*
c. *Scruples*
d. *Flamingo Road*

Answer: b

7 "THE ATTITUDE"
Original Airdate: November 3, 1997

Ally takes a client who can't get a get (Jewish divorce) from her comatose ex-husband because her rabbi (Jason Blicker) refuses. So Ally gives him some attitude, ridicules his religious beliefs, and he calls her "bitchy"–apparently this sounds like romance. Meanwhile Georgia joins the firm after (surprise!) successfully suing her former employer for discrimination.

COMMENTARY

As far as Ally sex-capades go, this may as well be the swingin', free-love episode, what with our heroine getting to date a rabbi and a loser who gets salad dressing on his chin. Personally, we wish she'd kept dating that sassy holy man all season. But Ally's continual mixing up of "mistletoe" and "mazel tov"? C'mon, nobody's that white bread.

VERDICT

MCTRIVIA

In "The Attitude" former tampon pitchwoman Brenda Vaccaro plays Ally's client. She played a different kind of client altogether in which movie?

a. *Shampoo*
b. *American Gigolo*
c. *The Love Machine*
d. *Midnight Cowboy*

Answer: d

8 "DRAWING THE LINES"
Original Airdate: November 10, 1997

There's a big money divorce case, but the real action is in the Unisex when (first Ally, then Georgia, now . . .) Elaine cries sexual harassment because the guys keep ogling busty Jennifer the mail girl (Brooke Burns)—not her. Ally and Georgia watch in disgust as Billy and Fish go into a trance at the sight of Jennifer, then retire to Ally's office for an unusual lesson: Ally sensuously shows Georgia how to enjoy her cappuccino like sexual foreplay. Unfortunately for Georgia, this reminds Billy of sexual foreplay . . . with Ally!

COMMENTARY

Ally's not the first show we've seen tackle sexual foreplay, food, and the big O. Some "little death" pioneers of film and TV are: When Harry Met Sally, in which Meg Ryan serenaded the patrons of a New York deli with a "coming-right-up" they hadn't expected (Herbal Essences shampoo spoofs the scene in its ads); the famous Seinfeld "Master of My Domain" episode (are you the master of your domain?); Fast Times at Ridgemont High, in which a slinky Phoebe Cates showed Jennifer Jason Leigh how to perform oral sex with a banana; and the Great Granddaddy of all sex 'n' eats scenes, 9 1/2 Weeks, where viewers wondered why Kim Basinger—and Mickey Rourke—didn't just climb into the fridge to cool themselves off. This Ally McBeal, halfway between the Playboy channel and a call-in show with Dr. Ruth, is the perfect venue to carry on this proud tradition. On top of that piping hot cappuccino-gasm, we get extra chocolate comedy sprinkles in the form of Sandra Bernhard, which makes up for the boring divorce case.

VERDICT

MCTRIVIA

In "Drawing the Lines" wild and crazy entertainment juggernaut Sandra Bernhard plays Elaine's lawyer, Caroline Poop. What was the name of her critically acclaimed off-Broadway one-woman show?

a. *Truth or Dare*
b. *Without You I'm Nothing*
c. *Sandra Bernhard Live!*
d. *The Queen of Comedy*

Answer: b

9 "THE DIRTY JOKE"
Original Airdate: November 17, 1997

Holy Clarence Thomas! Now it's buxom Jennifer the mail girl's turn to sue for sexual harassment because Elaine's complaint created a "hostile work environment." Caroline Poop is on the scene again as her lawyer . . . and Georgia worries that Poop's making passes at her. Apologies to 13-year-old boys everywhere, but the real reason Caroline can't help staring is because she's never seen a "living Barbie doll."

COMMENTARY

Lesbians! Barbie dolls! Big alabaster boobies! (As Elaine calls Jennifer's breasts.) All that, plus Ally trying to stop getting labeled a "Julie Andrews" by telling a dirty joke. It seems you can't turn the channel without bumping into a lesbian these days . . . and boy, is Howard Stern happy about it. Pump up the Melissa Etheridge and K.D. Lang, pop in a copy of Mr. Wrong, *and become acquainted with the works of Sarah Schulman. (Want to dress for same-sex viewing success? It's not really true that all lesbians look like those girls in* Bound, *but they do look cool, don't they? Try the undershirt look, go gamine, or pop on some spike heels and roll on the Revlon. Also make sure you've stocked up on at least twenty different kinds of Celestial Seasonings.) Whatever you're wearing, this "celluloid docket" Ally is a humdinger.*

VERDICT

MCTRIVIA

Julie Andrews tried to get over being labeled a "Julie Andrews" by waving her big alabaster boobies in our faces in what movie?

a. *The Man Who Loved Women*
b. *Thoroughly Modern Milly*
c. *S.O.B.*
d. *10*

Answer: c

> ### HAS CAGE/FISH & ASSOCIATES EVER LOST A CASE?
> This isn't *Perry Mason*—although their record is pretty good. The firm has lost three cases so far:
>
> 1. Ally lost her first case in the pilot (but was redeemed on appeal)
> 2. Judge Whipper dealt the firm's polygamist clients a blow in "Silver Bells"
> 3. John Cage lost the case of the mad paddle-whacker to Renee Radick in the season finale, "These Are the Days."

10 "BOY TO THE WORLD"
Original Airdate: December 7, 1997

Okay, some fans love this "very special *Ally McBeal*" in which Ally befriends a young transvestite prostitute who (surprise!) ends up getting murdered. A more lighthearted subplot concerns Richard Fish's desire to honor his late uncle by mentioning the man's hatred of short people at the funeral.

COMMENTARY

Putting "very special" before anything is like sticking a tongue-depressor down one's throat; even a "very special Ally McBeal" can't help but cause a little gagging. (Fans of "very special" episodes probably also groove out on the contrived, maudlin plots of Sisters.*) Here the funeral subplot is less cloying, but Jennifer Holliday and Randy Newman-singing gospel choirs aside, this shtick feels like a pale rehash of "The Affair."*

VERDICT

MCTRIVIA

While he played transvestite Stephanie in "Boy to the World," actor Wilson Cruz is best known as Angela's gay buddy on *My So-Called Life*. What was his character's name?

a. Ricky
b. Darrell
c. Manuel
d. Lucas

Answer: a

11 "SILVER BELLS"
Original Airdate: December 1, 1997

Ally represents James, Mindy and Pattie Horton, who would like to be legally married—to each other. Whipper puts pressure on Fish to get married, and everybody has a good time at the office holiday party, except Cage, who is filled with anxiety over whether or not he's good dating material.

COMMENTARY

Ah, the heretofore undiscovered country of the ménage à trois. Or maybe not—it seems we're seeing TV triangles everywhere we look, and not just on Three's Company *(which had at least one character either having to hide in the bathroom, bedroom or kitchen in every episode to avoid a roommate's honey). The teens of* Dawson's Creek *are way ahead of their time with Dawson, Joey, and Jen locked in a battle of affections; Alexis, Crystal and Blake may have shattered a store's worth of wine glasses with the venom of their* Dynasty *trio; Melrose's Allison took two seasons to discover that boss Amanda meant more than extra flow charts when she said she'd be "working closely" with Allison's boyfriend Billy; and* The Brady Bunch *broke the bank with three—count 'em—three sets of trios: Marsha, Jan and Cindy; Peter, Bobby and Greg; and Carol, Mike and Alice (well, in spirit, anyway). The polygamy plot in this episode is pure poppycock—a thin excuse to hear more about the polyamorous Ally, Billy, and Georgia—but luckily this episode also features Elaine, with backup "Ikettes" Richard and Renee, belting it out at the office party. Surprise, surprise . . . it's Fish's jazzy number that steals the show . . . .*

VERDICT

 *Last time we checked, multiple marriage was illegal, and Ally's stolen kiss with Cage under the mistletoe is a big downer—why's she leading him on?*

MCTRIVIA

In what year did federal law specifically outlaw polygamy?

a. 1890
b. 1916
c. 1725
d. 1933

Answer: a

12 "CRO-MAGNON"
Original Airdate: January 5, 1998

Ally is haunted by that dancing baby, the living embodiment of her biological clock. What's a stressed-out yuppie to do? Make time to take an evening sculpture class with Renee and Georgia! The gals gossip about Glenn (Michael Easton), an artist's model with extraordinary gifts. Billy overhears and is stricken with a mean case of penis anxiety.

COMMENTARY

What the heck is Billy worried about? He's got two babes throwing themselves at him! Extraordinary Glenn's assets aside, the real star of this episode is Baby Cha-cha, whose debut became one of the most talked-about television stories of the year. Ooga-chaka!

VERDICT

MCTRIVIA:

Viennese spinmeister Sigmund Freud promulgated the controversial "penis envy" theory. Who was his most famous—and dreamy—disciple?

a. William James
b. Jean-Luc Godard
c. Doctor Ruth
d. Carl Jung

Answer: d

13 "THE BLAME GAME"
Original Airdate: January 19, 1997

After sleeping with her twice, Glenn leaves Ally because he thinks she's only using him for sex–which is true, sort of. Still, hell hath no fury like an Ally scorned. Our vengeful heroine joins forces with Renee and Georgia to employ the neutron bomb of revenge pranks: the Penguin. Renee tricks Glenn into pulling his pants down in public, and Ally slams Billy for calling her promiscuous.

COMMENTARY

Ouch! Ally gets tossed in the Dumpster again. But promiscuous? Hello, where has Billy been? Ally's had sex twice in five months, and suddenly she's promiscuous? Billy deserves to get screamed at for that one, but we still feel bad for what she did to poor Glenn. It's also interesting to think how if all of the women in the world assembled the collective prank-lore we've gathered over the centuries (a mass Washington Penguin, anyone?) we could take over Congress in a flash. Get your buds together and make up a little black book for those times when you try to say "Man," but it keeps coming out, "Dog." And never show it to the uninitiated.

VERDICT

MCTRIVIA

Which actor played the Penguin on the Batman TV show?

a. Ernest Borgnine
b. Cesar Romero
c. Burgess Meredith
d. Phil Leeds

Answer: c

14 "BODY LANGUAGE"
Original Airdate: February 2, 1998

The Biscuit extols the benefits of "smile therapy," grinning blankly in times of stress, and Fish flirts with Janet Reno at the bar. In yet another quirky Cage/Fish sex case, Ally and Georgia wind up getting pulled over while ferrying a cup of a prisoner's semen to his fiancée in a harebrained artificial insemination scheme.

COMMENTARY

We never really thought about the cup-method before, but taking a closer look at some of the men Ally is supposed to date, this artificial insemination routine doesn't seem a half-bad idea. If artificial insemination had existed in the days of Lucy & Ethel, it's easy to imagine the two flinging around "cold cups" instead of Hershey's kisses. But Janet Reno hanging out with strange men in martini bars? All in all, pretty pedestrian Ally.

VERDICT

MCTRIVIA

Where did Janet Reno attend law school?

a. NYU
b. Harvard
c. Berkeley
d. Stanford

Answer: b

15 "ONCE IN A LIFETIME"
Original Airdate: February 23, 1998

Cage gets advice from his colleagues on curbing his saliva flow in anticipation of kissing Ally on her mercy date with him, which, naturally, turns out to be a disaster. In court, Ally defends a scrappy old windbag of an artist played by Richard Kiley who battles his son over the right to sell paintings of his dead wife.

COMMENTARY

Mmwa! The sloppy kiss episode. We'd much rather get a big, wet sloppy kiss from Cage (why can't the poor guy get a date? He's not married, and he's not Fish . . .) than sit through a tired Hallmark Hall of Fame about a kooky codger whose true love was (brace yourself) "Once in a Lifetime." This leads Ally and Billy to ponder their own "Once in a Lifetime" liaison. Yada yada yada.

VERDICT

MCTRIVIA

Veteran actor Richard Kiley played crackers painter Seymour Little in "Once in a Lifetime." Kiley costarred with a creature in what film?

a. *Howard the Duck*
b. *Benji*
c. *The Yearling*
d. *Harry and the Hendersons*

Answer: a

16 "FORBIDDEN FRUITS"
Original Airdate: March 2, 1998

Ally defends a U.S. senator who's being sued by his wife's first husband for breaking up their marriage. Opposing counsel is Anna Flint, whose dazzling smile is legendary. The trial love triangle talk is too much for Georgia, who blurts out what we've all been thinking: that Ally and Billy ought to just–well, get this burning, yearning thing out of their systems.

COMMENTARY

Luckily for us, Ally and Billy are smart enough not to repeat the mistakes made in Moonlighting *and don't take Georgia up on her suggestion, though they actually have the nerve to act shocked at the suggestion they've both been fantasizing about. Whoever said lawyers were untrustworthy? This episode also infuriated many feminists with Ally's courtroom "smile off" against aggressive attorney Anna Flint.*

VERDICT

 *Bonus points for Anna Flint slamming Ally's hemlines.*

MCTRIVIA

Dina Meyer, the actress who is nasty lawyer Anna Flint in "Forbidden Fruits," played Kate, a recurring character on what NBC sitcom?

a. *Frasier*
b. *Suddenly Susan*
c. *The Naked Truth*
d. *Friends*

Answer: d

17 "THEME OF LIFE"
Original Airdate: March 9, 1998

Ally falls for Dr. Greg Butters, who's being sued for sticking a pig's liver in a patient, and squares off against Georgia in a kickboxing match, and Whipper dumps Fish over another Janet Reno indiscretion. Best of all, our heroine finally gets therapy—from the truly demented Dr. Tracey Clark.

COMMENTARY

To one and all, this is the "theme song" episode, in which Ally decides that "Tell Him" will be her anthem and gets an entire crowd of commuters rocking with her. Actually, we prefer Dr. Tracey's goofy theme tune—"Tracy" by the Cuff Links. Interestingly, the name—and song—were chosen before Tracey Ullman was cast in the role. When she was, David Kelley briefly considered changing the character's name but didn't want to give up that song. Since we're not the editors of Jane magazine, we're not going to suggest that you take kickboxing or, God forbid, actually hold a kickboxing match. But we do suggest that you rent the preeminent kickboxing movie of all time, Say Anything, and think about the fact that Cusack is Greek for "The most adorable man in the entire history of the world."

VERDICT

 *One of the best shows of the season.*

MCTRIVIA

Tracey Ullman's very own theme song is Kristy MacColl's "They Don't Know." As a pop single it gave the English actress and comedienne her first taste of American success. It hit the charts in what year?

a. 1982
b. 1981
c. 1984
d. 1985

Answer: c

18 "THE PLAYING FIELD"
Original Airdate: March 16, 1998

Dr. Tracey tells Ally to cut the whining and kick Mr. Huggy in the patootie when next they meet. Unfortunately she accidentally kicks 9-year-old little person and child prodigy lawyer Oren Koolie instead. Too bad he's suing her new man, Dr. Butters. There's also another sex harassment suit, this time from a woman who claims she lost out because her boss *didn't* sleep with her.

COMMENTARY

Who hasn't wanted to kick a child prodigy at some point? They're arrogant know-it-alls who always act like such ... children. (Also, anything you can do, they can do better.) That's why a quick viewing of Amadeus, Shine, *or any episode of* Doogie Howser, M.D. *will help reassure you that while child prodigies may have the grey matter where it counts, they still can't drink, smoke, or have sex. Unfortunately, you don't drink or smoke. Shall we go on? But if you watch this rerun in high-heels and a pinstripe suit, then go out to the fanciest restaurant you can find and put it on your Visa (which is ten dollars away from being overdrawn) you might get over it: remember, goddamnit, you're the grown-up! Also, Gloria Steinem probably loved Richard Fish's speech about how women should be covered under the Americans with Disabilities Act because they can't handle office romance as much as Georgia did—but Ally's own imaginary backup singers, the Ally Pips, prove that sisterhood really is powerful.*

VERDICT

 Three gavels for three Ally Pips.

MCTRIVIA

Recently, the Spice Girls rocked the house as arguably the most famous girl group of all time. Which up-and-coming girl group is hot on their heels?

a. All Saints
b. The Crystals
c. The Raincoats
d. En Vogue

Answer: a

EPISODE 18 INSIDE JOKE ALERT:
Ally refers to Koolie as "Doogie Munchkin." As you know if you've been paying attention, *Doogie Howser, M.D.* was also spawned by none other than the tireless Lord of All Things Ally, David Kelley.

19 "HAPPY BIRTHDAY, BABY"
Original Airdate: April 6, 1998

Ally's birthday episode, in which she has a very unsympathetic complex about turning . . . 28 (boo-hoo-hoo). To mark this dark day, she gets serenaded by Vonda, Elaine and the soulful Dr. Greg, who's a great guy she ends up dumping, anyway. (All together now: "'Cause I'm a WOMAN . . .") To get over the breakup, Ally fatally beats up the one steady guy in her life: her beloved inflatable man. She also gets to defend Mark Anderson, a foot fetishist.

COMMENTARY

Who knew that Elaine's need for attention came from the fact that she hadn't gotten a bike as a child? (No one.) Who knew that underneath Elaine's hair she was actually a very sad, lonely person? (Well, you did, probably.) Yet another fetish show (lessee—wattles, teeth, women's clothing, the smell of denim, feet . . .). And things get even kinkier when as a trial negotiating tactic, Ally massages prosecutor Renee Radick's feet, sending the DA into orgiastic rapture—making us wonder if Ally's soul mate ain't her roommate. . . .

VERDICT

MCTRIVIA

In this episode Ally turns 28, making her how many years younger than actress Calista Flockhart (if, unlike Calista, you believe available records)?

a. 6
b. 10
c. 5
d. 3

Answer: c

20 "THE INMATES"
Originally Aired: April 27, 1998

The firm takes on a gory murder case in which a wife whacks her husband, perhaps because she thinks she's the reincarnation of Lizzie Borden, and turns to criminal lawyer Bobby Donnelly (Dylan McDermott) for help. Renee accidentally breaks her date's neck when he manhandles her, and Fish takes on a gay discrimination case, with predictable results.

COMMENTARY

This is the Ally McBeal-The Practice *crossover, a fusion that broke all the rules—start a lawyer story on featherlight* Ally McBeal *on Fox, then commit heresy and continue the tale on competitor ABC, where the gritty* Practice *airs. It's a testament to the success of* Ally *that the meld took place over the protest of Fox affiliates–who threatened to yank the show, then chickened out. More memorable for the buzz than the plot, though it's fun to watch sparks fly between Ally and Bobby (Billy Shmilly—this is a man worthy of her daydreams).*

VERDICT

 *Mostly for Dylan McDermott.*

MCTRIVIA

In what movie did Dylan McDermott play opposite Julia Roberts?

a. *Sleeping with the Enemy*
b. *Steel Magnolias*
c. *Mystic Pizza*
d. *Dying Young*

Answer: b

21 | "BEING THERE"
Original Airdate: May 4, 1998

Bill! Georgia thinks she's pregnant, and a stressed-out Ally copes with the news by employing the goofy Fifth Dimension tune "Wedding Bell Blues" as a theme song, and the entire office joins in with an equally goofy Broadway-style production number. The Biscuit defends Renee against assault charges brought by the guy she bashed in "The Inmates," and Ally's feisty roomie admits that under her sexual bravado lies a lot of insecurity.

COMMENTARY

Remember Bernie Goetz? Renee's just one of a long line of people who, because of bad past experiences, sometimes overreact in the face of stress. (Although if you ask us, sometimes giving a guy a swift kick in the chin is just faster—and cheaper—than taking him to court. Though breaking his neck may be extreme, it's true ...) Renee's revelations about being teased for being an early bloomer are sweet enough, but it's really that Unisex kick line that makes this a gem.

VERDICT

MCTRIVIA

Which symbol is not a possible outcome of a home pregnancy test?

a. A + sign
b. A - sign
c. A ? sign
d. A = sign

Answer: c

22 "ALONE AGAIN"
Original Airdate: May 11, 1998

Ally and Cage work on the case of 72-year-old Vincent Robbins, who one month before his 18-year prison sentence is up makes a rubber band trampoline and escapes . . . temporarily. In the process Cage locks horns with DA Hayley Chisolm, an old law school chum who's practically his distaff twin (she takes Lamaze classes, although there's nary a bun in the oven). It's clear that he's head over heels—and so is Fish, who tries to make up with Whipper.

COMMENTARY

Cage's closing argument subtly comparing Robbins's leap over the prison wall to his own wish to declare his feelings to Hayley makes this episode a winner. Like Star Trek's Data, *it's not often that we get to see the Poughkeepsie-humming, toilet-flushing, moment-taking Cage loosen up, show his feelings and break out of his "Cage" instead of hiding himself behind a wall of quirks. This is one soppy Ally McMoment that works—during this scene goofy Cage almost gives sexy Billy a run for his money.*

VERDICT

MCTRIVIA

Cynthia Stevenson is perhaps best known as the star of the short-lived sitcom *Hope & Gloria*. In 1992 she was cast in another canceled show as Trish McKay, the daughter of which famous Hollywood comedian?

a. Bob Newhart
b. George Carlin
c. Martin Mull
d. Fred Willard

Answer: a

CLOSING ARGUMENTS

As you probably noticed, the signature logo of David Kelley's production company is an old lady who shouts, "You stinkah!" in a thick Boston accent at the end of every episode of *Ally McBeal*. What's the McDeal? It's a tribute to Kelley's 97-year-old grandmother, who on occasion has been known to call him by his childhood nickname: Stinker.

23 "THESE ARE THE DAYS"
Original Airdate: May 18, 1998

The season finale of Ally McBeal gets a hunk infusion from returning guest star Dylan McDermott, who works with Ally on a case involving two men who want an operation to switch hearts. The Biscuit loses a case involving a cousin who whacks couples on the head with a canoe paddle to "help" them fall in love. Not needing any help are Georgia and Billy, whom Ally surprises doing the nasty in the conference room.

COMMENTARY

Is Ally spraying herself with Off instead of Enjoli? Bobby smooches her and then says distance, maybe because the commute from ABC is murder (time for the Penguin again?). At least Renee has a reason to smile—she finally wins a court case by whupping the Biscuit in the canoe-whacker trial. For all McDermott-philes: It's like Tinkerbell in Peter Pan. *If you say, "I Believe! (that Fox should have Dylan McDermott return to Allyland as often as possible") then the beloved Dylan will live to see another season. Rent* Hamburger Hill *and* Steel Magnolias; *dig up "Blood on the Tracks" and your Wallflowers CD; and take turns reading from the works of Dylan Thomas. And believe.*

VERDICT

MCTRIVIA

Having sex in public is one of the fastest ways to give someone (besides the two participants) a heart attack. On what sitcom did a couple threaten to have public sex to shock—and lure—viewers away from the famous final *Seinfeld* episode?

a. *Spin City*
b. *Homicide*
c. *Buffy the Vampire Slayer*
d. *Dharma and Greg*

ALLY OOPS: Tort Reform

Allyworld is a peculiar place that operates with its own laws—even about the Law. Here's three instances that never would have occurred outside of TV:

1. In "Drawing the Lines," Elaine claims that *not* being ogled is a form of sexual harassment. Traditional harassment claims must include either an individual overture or a hostile environment. Since Elaine can't claim either, the suit she files against the firm would be groundbreaking—and extremely difficult to prove.

2. In "The Dirty Joke," Caroline Poop represents first Elaine, then Jennifer, the mail girl. In real life, Caroline would have been disqualified from representing Jennifer: as Elaine's lawyer, she may have learned information about the firm from her client that she would not be permitted to use in Jennifer's case.

3. In "Silver Bells," the firm takes on the case of a ménage à trois that wants to be made legal in the eyes of the state. Hello—credibility demerits for allowing a civil court judge to hear a polygamy case.

One Fish Is Enough Fish

Richard Fish is entirely amoral, venal, self-promoting and vain, which makes it very hard not to love him. Fresh out of law school, he started a practice to make "piles and piles" of money (though we've never heard how he got all the money to start it). In the courtroom he's an unmitigated embarrassment to the firm, but in the Unisex, he's always a hoot.

First, there's those Fishisms, those self-serving pearls of wisdom designed to justify his nearly always beastly behavior. And then there's that unhealthy fixation with women's wattles—ugh. No wonder Ally hated him in law school. But like her, we've discovered that Richard can be a hopelessly endearing fellow. Capable of sensitivity, even. Like the time he apologized to the firm mail girl for drooling over her alabaster boobies every time she walked by, or delivered his uncle's eulogy (granted, it was a eulogy about his uncle's hatred of short people). And despite his avowed commitment phobia, he's clearly devoted to more than just Whipper's wattle—at least as long as his pinup girl Janet Reno stays away from Boston.

In playing Fish, Greg Germann gets to be our collective id—a hilariously politically incorrect scamp who dares to say what many don't even dare think. He's also become a cult hero in the process. But what of all those pre-Fish years spent slogging away in thankless best-buddy roles? Ah, well. Bygones.

THEY IMMIGRATED FROM GUR-MANY

Greg was born in Houston, Texas, and raised in the suburbs of Denver. His family name is pronounced with a hard g, and given that the moniker probably didn't make Granddad Mr. Popularity in 1942, who can blame them?

THEY SAID YOU WERE AN ARTISTE . . .

After majoring in theater at the University of Northern Colorado, Greg went to New York, where he became a member of the Circle Rep and Ensemble theater companies, and appeared in critically acclaimed plays by David Mamet, Stephen Sondheim and Neil Simon.

. . . BUT THAT WAS A LIE

When not pounding the boards, Greg played "Creepy" in the 1984 hooker-exploitation picture *Streetwalkin'*, appeared in the zipper-level *The Whoopee Boys*, shared the screen with . . .

GREG GERMANN

"Hey, look, I love him. He's paying the rent."
—*Greg Germann commenting on his relationship with Fish,*
in USA Today

Howard Rosenberg/Shooting Star

HOLLY-WOOD CALLING

Greg has appeared in two Holly Hunter movies—as hick Ronnie Wayne in *Miss Firecracker* and Jim Redstone in *Once Around*, which was about an uptight single girl in Boston . . . sound familiar?

LITTLE COURTHOUSE ON THE PRAIRIE

Before *Ally McBeal*, Greg was a regular on the forgettable Melissa Gilbert Boxleitner lawyer show *Sweet Justice*. He also played an assistant DA in the TV movie *Taking the Heat* and, like Courtney Thorne-Smith, guest-starred on *L.A. Law*.

AND YOU THOUGHT FISH WAS CLUELESS

Before a certain groundbreaking episode, and back when the show was called *These Friends of Mine*, Greg was cast as Rick, a neighbor with a huge crush on . . . Ellen DeGeneres.

. . . killer doll Chucky in *Child's Play 2*, and was a clerk in the Mike Myers stinker *So I Married an Axe Murderer*. Greg finally escaped the clear and present danger of being relegated to the rental video bargain bin by landing a small role in the Harrison Ford action pic *Clear and Present Danger*.

WONDER WHAT *SHE'D* THINK OF A JUDGE WITH A TOOTH FETISH

Before spawning Fish, Greg was

GLOBE PHOTOS

best known as a supporting character on the Fox comedy *Ned and
Stacey*. Stacey was Debra Messing,
who also played Jerry's rabidly anti-
Dentite girlfriend Beth in the infamous "Yada Yada Yada" episode of
Seinfeld.

THEIR VERY OWN LITTLE ROE

Greg is married to actress and
Vonda-esque singer/songwriter
Christine Mourad. They also have
a son, Asa.

IF GREG GERMANN HAD A THEME SONG, IT WOULD BE

... "I am Germann, Here Me Roar"

THE TOP 10
REASONS THE WORLD'S

1. HE'S A POPULIST

"Let's face it—I'm upper-ordinary, not extraordinary—never will be!"

2. HE'S A HUMANITARIAN

"Helping people is never more rewarding than when it's in your own self-interest."

3. HE'S BRUTALLY HONEST

"I'm nothing if not redundant. I also repeat myself."

4. HE BELIEVES IN THE AMERICAN WAY

"It's not just winning—it's winning ugly that matters."

5. HE'S A *RULES* BOY

"If you don't kiss a girl on the first date, you are a gentleman. If you don't kiss her on the second, you are gay."

GONE FISHIN'

6. HE'S ZEN
"Make enough money, and everything else will follow."

7. HE'S A MOTIVATIONAL SPEAKER
"*Problem* is just a bleak word for *challenge*."

8. HE'S A HOPELESS ROMANTIC
"Love is an equation. A me and a you derives a we."

9. HE'S GOT SCHOOL SPIRIT
"Reunions are meant to allow the more successful graduates to inform the less successful that is what they are, less than. You and I are more than. Especially me. I've got my own firm. I could possibly be the most."

10. HE'S HAUNTED BY HIS CONSCIENCE
"One of the keys to life is fast-forward. Every movie has its lousy parts. The trick is to fast-forward through them. As time passes you look back and say, 'Oh, that little adultery thing. Oh, that.' Fast-forward to then, right now, and you are over it."

An-Ally-Sis

Despite urging from concerned (and perhaps aggrieved) parties, Ally didn't go rushing to a therapist's couch—she liked being a mess very much, thank you. But eventually she took the advice of John Cage and went to his analyst, Dr. Tracey Clark, to rummage through her baggage. Though Lord knows why she would take advice on therapy from quite possibly the most unbalanced man in Massachusetts.

What, if any, credentials does Dr. Tracey have? Is she a Freudian or a Jungian? Her entire treatment method seems to consist of the following: Hum a few bars of Burt Bacharach and call me in the morning. Amazingly, that hasn't been bad advice—Ally's first theme song, "Tell Him," and her pick-me-up number, "Wedding Bell Blues," seemed to chase everybody in Boston's blues away. Compare the good head-doctor's advice with that of some of her colleagues, and you'll see she doesn't come off as half-bad.

MENTAL CRISIS
"I imagine I am swimming in a cup of coffee with my married ex-boyfriend."

THERAPIST'S ADVICE
Dr. Tracey Clark: Dunk the bastard.
Dr. Laura Schlesinger: If you aren't married, grab on to a doughnut chunk and dog-paddle the heck out of there.
Dr. Ruth: Is he wearing a condom?
Dr. Sigmund Freud: The warm steamy cup symbolizes your desire to return to your mother's comforting womb.

MENTAL CRISIS
"Whenever a man breaks up with me, I picture myself being tossed into a Dumpster by a garbage truck."

THERAPIST'S ADVICE
Dr. Tracey Clark: Dust yourself off, and go ask that garbage man for a date!
Dr. Laura Schlesinger: If you are sleeping around, you deserve to be treated like garbage, you selfish little tramp.
Dr. Ruth: If you are going to make love in the Dumpster, make sure he wears a condom.
Dr. Sigmund Freud: The garbage truck is your mother, the shovel is her vagina—you resent her pushing you from her warm, steamy comfortable womb into the distasteful world symbolized by the Dumpster.

MENTAL CRISIS
"In times of stress at work, I picture myself drowning."

THERAPIST'S ADVICE
Dr. Tracey Clark: Buy a wet suit and pretend you're with Keanu Reeves in *Point Break*!
Dr. Laura Schlesinger: All career women are drowning, and it's your own fault for buying into feminazi family-wrecking mumbo jumbo. I wish I were there to tie cinder blocks to your selfish little ankles.
Dr. Ruth: Saltwater is not an adequate contraceptive!
Dr. Sigmund Freud: Are you wearing a bikini?

MENTAL CRISIS
"When something cruel is said to me, I often see an arrow piercing my heart."

THERAPIST'S ADVICE
Dr. Tracey Clark: Turn yourself into Wonder Woman and deflect the arrow with your magic Amazonian bracelets.
Dr. Laura Schlesinger: Move a little to the left next time so I can get a better shot.
Dr. Ruth: If piercing feels painful, try changing your lubricant.
Dr. Sigmund Freud: Sometimes an arrow is just an arrow.

MENTAL CRISIS
"I am haunted by an animated dancing baby."

THERAPIST'S ADVICE
Dr. Tracey Clark: Hog-tie the sucker and go about your merry way!
Dr. Laura Schlesinger: If you had any sense of decency, you'd put that baby up for adoption.
Dr. Ruth: Was this baby conceived through unsafe sex?
Dr. Sigmund Freud: If you look closer, you'll see the baby is really a short Viennese man.

DOROTHY HANDELMAN

Sex and the (can you believe she's still...) Single Girl

Take one look at her and it's obvious: Ally's a knockout. Okay, she's a little bit underfed, but that could just be her metabolism. She shouldn't have any problem finding a man, and yet she does.

Certainly a lot of this has to do with the big B-man still being in her life. But we reckon that even if Billy got taken out in a drive-by tomorrow, Ally wouldn't be any closer to finding Mr. Right. She's a picky little thing, you know. Even if she had Billy, she probably wouldn't be happy with him. Sure, for the first couple of days he'd be okay, but then he'd dribble ranch dressing all over her Turkish kilim or smoke a cigar in bed, and before you know it, even her destined-since-birth soul mate would be one big turnoff.

Like many of us, Ally's just more satisfied being dissatisfied. Sometimes she'll go so far as to admit that it's the chase that really excites her, not the big, jockstrap-wearing quarry. In that way she's like a lot of people out there—a fair number of them being, you know, men.

If Ally could get NIH funding, she might build her own man, using bits of her exes' personalities and handy bits of reanimated tissue (thanks, Glenn). But even then she'd still probably find some flaws. After all, she's in the love game for the dreaming, not the dreamboats.

> *"Ally McBeal is a mess. She's like a little animal. You want to put her on a leash."*
> —Nancy Friday, *being a little catty, in* Time

A GROOM OF ONE'S OWN

Since Ally's dated a rabbi, a Supreme Court clerk, a male model, and Hercules among other stand-up guys, the sum of their individual parts would be pretty indeed. We bring you super-Ally man (Or to quote a certain Transylvanian doctor . . . it lives!):

HAIR: The late Jack Dawson was in the thick of middle age when he dated Ally and he was blessed with a nice, fluffy headful of blond-gray thatch. Good hair gene, bad heart gene.

SMILE: His kisses knocked Ally off her feet, but maybe there's something to the Biscuit's smile therapy thing . . .

VOICE: Dr. Greg Butters sings like buttah. The very sound of his voice makes women melt. And he's good at pig-to-human transplant surgery too!

FACE: Bobby Donnelly may have an ugly law practice, but his kisser always pleases the court.

BRAIN: Ally doesn't generally date morons (well, there was Glenn), but of all the men in her life, the one who'd provide the best wattage would be....9 year old genius lawyer Oren Koolie. All right, they didn't *exactly* date. But she did let him sit on her lap.

HEART: Okay, he's happily married, but we know when it comes to Ally, Billy's heart is always in the right place. Let her keep the rest of him. Especially the hair. We certainly wouldn't want Jack Dawson's bum ticker.

SEWING ABILITY: Stephanie, the ill-fated cross-dressing call boy Ally tried to rescue, clearly had a lot of problems, but he could whip up a mean black dress. He could design Ally a closet full of his "Freudian slips."

BUTT: Anyone of Ally's sculpted boy-toys would do here, but for the sake of sweet revenge, the honor should go to lard-ass Jack Billings, the boss who couldn't keep his hands off her tush. That way she could grab *his* butt all day . . .

TALLYWHACKER: Winner by more than a yard—Glenn, the snowboarding artist's model. Sorry Billy, she lied. It does matter.

HUGGABILITY: Until she popped him, Ally's inflatable man was always there for a comforting squeeze.

ARMS, LEGS, LOWER BACKS: The Ally-Pips. For all the heavy lifting (not to mention emotional valida-tion), you can never have too many Pips around the house.

DANCING SHOES: Who else but that Polyester pair, the dancing twins?

WALLET: For this and nothing else (certainly not the mouth), Richard. He loves loot, and we just know he has his piles and piles stashed away somewhere.

SENSE OF HUMOR: To answer Ally's point-ed question to the good Rabbi Stern, yes God does love the bitchy. And this Rabbi loves the bitchy, too. His sharp wit makes him a shoe-in the borscht-belt category.

CONSCIENCE: Richard Cheanie wasn't much of a kisser, but his strong moral core appealed to Ally. Apparently the only man in Boston who knows prostitution is demeaning and illegal.

SWINGLE SISTERS

When Ellen came out of the closet on network TV, the family values crowd did plenty of hollering about her Sodom-and-Gomorrah takeover of Middle America, but they missed a far more vast and ancient Sapphic conspiracy, lurking just beneath the cover of your *TV Guide*. Unbeknownst to Flag-loving, God-fearing Americans everywhere, committed lesbian couples have colonized our television sets.

Take Renee and Ally. Here are two beautiful, successful, single women, and they complain they can't find a steady man? Why, of course. Because they are already going steady, and we didn't need the foot-massage episode to tell us that. And this being a show produced by David "push-the-envelope" Kelley, it could be only a matter of time before the happy pair are off to Honolulu for a commitment ceremony.

To most backsliding, morally bankrupt, secular humanist fans of *Ally McBeal*, that might sound like a lot of fun. But say you weren't warned. Sure, it starts out harmlessly enough, with a pair of 35-year-old gals sharing a room with twin beds. Next thing you know, the whole country's buying Indigo Girls records. Coincidence? Check out these exemplars of prime time Lesbian Chic:

Lucy & Ethel
- Shared penchant for matching coveralls and "Rosie the Riveter"-style head scarves
- Preferred swing shift at chocolate factory to homely arts
- Ethel married beard at least 20 years her senior; Lucy's marriage a green card scam
- Occasionally, Lucy dressed as man
- After leaving cosmopolitan New York City, pair never adjusted to life in uptight Connecticut suburbs

Mary & Rhoda
- Gave each other butch pet names "Mare" and "Rho"
- To live near each other, successful television executive Mary rented tiny studio apartment; successful window dresser Rhoda lived in broom closet
- Mary never had a man over; Rhoda never had man
- Occasionally Rhoda dressed as Long John Silver
- Smitten downstairs neighbor, "Phil," competed for Mary's attention and tried to break couple up

Kate & Allie
- Created "Heather Has Two Mommies"-style blended family
- Joined softball league
- Two words: Greenwich Village

- Allie displayed fondness for khaki pants; Kate displayed fondness for shag haircuts
- Allie assumed "femme" homemaker role; Kate cleaned gutters

Laverne & Shirley
- Two words: bottle cappers
- Wore matching mannish haircuts

- Shared bedroom for nearly a decade
- Took vacations with long-time companions Lenny and Squiggy
- Moved from conservative Midwest to southern California to escape prying eyes of Laverne's traditional Italian American father

Renee & Ally
- "Rene" and "Ali" very popular men's names in other countries
  - Most time in shared apartment spent snuggling in PJs
  - Renee broke man's neck when he got fresh
  - Grown women enjoy single sex "slumber parties" and invite only two guests
  - Ally gives Renee erotic foot massages that send her into uncontrolled fits of passion

We're gonna do it!

Lawyers in Love

"I've tried like hell to make bad movies good. And I can't."
—McDermott on his checkered film career

*Dreamy
Dylan*

Unlike its sister show, *Ally McBeal*, David Kelley's other lawyer show, *The Practice*, struggled longer to find an audience; perhaps because from the start, it wasn't a sunny, innovative take on the genre but a more traditional highbrow teledrama in a field crowded with them—from *Law & Order* to *Homicide*.

And yet *The Practice* is innovative. For starters, it focuses on the day-to-day work of criminal defense attorneys. To Fish, such attorneys are "bottom feeding scum suckers," but of course, you can't completely trust him for an opinion. The most popular lawyer shows on television feature prosecutors as heroes, not the defenders of the mostly guilty. It's dramatically far more complex territory, and the show has justifiably won praise for tackling it.

So when the two shows fused for one week last spring, critics were puzzled how Ally's yin would jibe with *The Practice*'s yang. Clearly, much of the motivation for the coupling was to rub a little McBuzz off on *The Practice*, and at least temporarily, the magic seems to have worked. More viewers are tuning into the somber, well-acted drama. Where *Ally* is essentially a comedy with dollops of drama, *The Practice* is the reverse. Although Fish would disagree, the actors do smile—they just don't do "smile therapy."

Like Calista Flockhart, Dylan McDermott is an engaging young actor with New York stage roots, but he's struggled for a decade to live up to the Next Big Thing tag earned after his film debut in the 1985 Vietnam War flick *Hamburger Hill*. *The Practice* may put McDermott permanently on Hollywood's A-List. While we wait and see, both he and Flockhart made *People*'s "50 Most Beautiful" list.

Ally McBeal and Bobby Donnelly clearly like the looks of one another, and his appearance on her show's season finale may signal that their relationship will percolate throughout the (hopefully) long runs of both their series. It's nice to see that mingling of yin and yang, dark and light, from time to time. A few notes on Mr. Tall Dark and Brooding, Esq.:

Next Stop, Greenwich Village:
Raised in Waterbury, Connecticut, by his grandmother, Dylan moved to New York to live with his father in the capital of Bohemia. He majored in theater at Fordham University, and was spied by an agent in a 1985 production of *Biloxi Blues* and cast in the critically acclaimed war movie *Hamburger Hill*.

"But Couldn't You Have Called it 'The Woo-Woo Monologues'?"
Dylan's stepmother is successful playwright Eve

EVERETT COLLECTION

Ensler, whom he credits with launching his acting career. When he was 17, she gave him his first role, in her play "Believe It, See It." There was no part for him in Ensler's *Vagina Monologues*, which were read by famous actresses in a benefit for Bosnian rape victims last year. One of the readers was Calista Flockhart.

"Hello, My Name Is Dylan, and Julia Dumped Me, Too."

After making a string of forgettable movies on the heels of *Hamburger Hill*, Dylan played Julia Roberts's love interest in the saccharine *Steel Magnolias*. After a whirlwind romance, the pair got engaged. Then Julia went off to film *Flatliners*, took up with Kieffer Sutherland, *they* got engaged, until she dumped Kieffer for . . . no, it's too painful. Can this heartbreaking hussy ever be stopped?

"Hello, My Name Is Dylan, and I Made *The Cowboy Way* Because Julia Dumped Me, Too."

After having his heart broken, Dylan made more forgettable films, and then got killed off but quick as Clint Eastwood's partner in *In the Line of Fire*. Things started looking up—but then he went and made the critically savaged "comedy" *The Cowboy Way* with . . . Kieffer Sutherland. No hard feelings, apparently.

And the Award for Best Acting in an Iron Lung Goes to . . .

After appearing in Jodie Foster's *Home for the Holidays*, Dylan romanced Jeanne Tripplehorn in *'Til There Was You*—a romantic comedy which was slammed for featuring characters chain smoking in nearly every scene. Like Fish, Dylan puffs ostentatiously on stogies.

TRULY A CREATURE UNLIKE ANY OTHER

We aren't proud of the fact that Ally has been caught consulting that frilly pink dating mini-festo known as *The Rules*, but nobody's perfect. Certainly Ally's not. But because she poked inside a Walgreens and grabbed a copy for some man-advice, does that mean she's a *Rules* girl?

Well, no. Ally's not consistent enough to be a *Rules* girl. Like with a busy law career and all those hallucinations she has time to get out a frilly pink marker and study *dating*—as June Cleaver would have practiced it? More importantly, we know from watching her for a year that while at weak moments Ally craves rules (or at least explanations) in life, most of the time she rebels against them. She isn't wearing thigh-high skirts in court because she's a follower. And she doesn't seem to like people who are smug, preachy, self-righteous or glassy-eyed. That rules out *Rules* girls.

We think, for all her flaws, Ally is far too smart to buy into a 12-step program that tells women to be quiet, look pretty, and dress in bright colors to attract men (see, like rutting bulls they're drawn . . . oh, never mind).

RULES GIRLS RULES

If you are in a long distance relationship with a man, he must visit you at least three times before you visit him

Never call a man, and rarely return his calls

Show up to parties and social events, even if you don't feel like it

It's a fantasy relationship unless a man asks you out

Close the deal—*Rules* women do not date men for more than two years

Take a bubble bath and build yourself up with powerful slogans like: "I am enough"

We're sure that even if she were tempted, Renee would kick her butt. But let's not get all dogmatic and *Rules*-girly. Ally's a contrary person—she might become a *Rules* girl just to bug us. That's part of what makes her real (antonym of *Rules* girl).What we like about her is she's a no-rules girl.

ALLY RULES

If you are in an imaginary relationship with a man, he must visit your subconscious three times before you visit his

Never call a man Stephanie

Show up to parties and social events, even if you don't feel like it, but let everybody know you don't feel like it, so they don't feel like it too. Then rent movie.

If you have good fantasies, you don't need to go out

Close the deal—women do not date married ex-boyfriends for more than two seasons

Take a Jell-O bath and build self up with powerful theme song like: "Tell Him"

Unusual Suspects

What's a quirky show without quirky guest stars? Why, it's the *Love Boat* without Charo—sailing around the Pacific with nobody to liven things up with a little coochie-coochie-coo on the lido deck. Charo hasn't yet appeared on *Ally McBeal*, though there's always next season. Meantime, these equally glamorous types are among the many that have:

Tate Donovan—Disney's Hercules played stick-in-the-mud Ronald Cheanie in "Compromising Positions," "The Affair," and "The Kiss."

Kate Jackson—Sensible Angel Sabrina "Brie" Duncan from *Charlie's Angels* and not-so sensible Mrs. King, from the *Scarecrow and Mrs. King*, played Barbara Cooker, an anchorwoman fired due to age discrimination, in "The Kiss."

Kathy Baker—Dr. Jill Brock of David Kelley's previous quirk-filled outing, as the widow of Ally's law professor—and ex-lover— in the "The Affair." She's one of many *Picket Fences* denizens who've showed up on the show, including her *Picket Fences* dad, Richard Kiley, as an artist in "Once in a Lifetime," and Christine Rose, who played her *Pickets* husband's ex-wife, in "Drawing the Lines."

EVERETT COLLECTION : © 20TH CENTURY FOX GLOBE PHOTOS

Actor Wilson Cruz, who played Ally's client Stephanie in "Boy to the World"

Sandra Bernhard—This glamorously guppy-mouthed star of stage, screen and David Letterman's couch played lawyer Caroline Poop in "Drawing the Lines" and "The Dirty Joke."

Wilson Cruz—Went from playing Angela and Raylene's troubled gay friend Ricky on *My So-Called Life* to playing Stephanie, Ally's troubled gay friend, in "Boy to the World."

Steve Harris, Lisa Gay Hamilton, Kelli Williams and Camryn Manheim—As those grumps from *The Practice* in "The Inmates."

Dreamgirl **Jennifer Holliday**—Led a gospel choir in a chorus of Randy Newman's "Short People" in "Boy to the World."

Jocko Marcellino—This lead singer from Sha-Na-Na greased it up as a prison guard in "These Are the Days."

Ralph Garcy—Of *Fame* fame. The Barry Miller, Freddie Prinz-lovin' comedian plays a foot-fetishist in "Happy Birthday, Baby." The object of his unwanted attention is **Harriet Sansom Harris**, the venomous talent agent from *Frasier*.

Two-time Tony winner **Donna Murphy**—As psycho-killer Mrs. Hanson in "The Inmates."

Peter Roth—The president of Fox Entertainment dances with Renee and tells her he runs a network on "Silver Bells."

Cynthia Stevenson—Hope on the hopeless *Hope & Gloria*, as Hayley, Cage's longtime crush.

Sassy Liz Torres—Best known as Mahalia on *The John Larroquette Show*, as the unwilling recipient of a pig's liver in "Theme of Life."

Tracey Ullman—Actress, comedian, and all-round madwoman, as Dr. Tracey Clark in "Theme of Life" and "The Playing Field."

Tampon saleswoman **Brenda Vaccaro**—As Karen Horowitz, who can't get a divorce from Rabbi Stern in "The Attitude."

Kathleen Wilhoite, formerly Chloe, Dr. Susan's druggie sister on *ER*, as the fiancee of a prisoner in "Body Language."

And on the bench . . . Veteran character actors **Phil Leeds** (from *The Exorcist* and *Dream On*) as judge Happy Boyle, **Alaina Reed Hall**, of *227*, as Judge Elizabeth Witt, and **Armin Shimerman** (Quark from *Star Trek: Deep Space Nine*) as Judge Walworth in "Boy to the World."

Bite the Biscuit!

When eccentric senior partner John Cage was introduced in the second episode of *Ally McBeal* fresh from being arrested for solicitation, he wasn't planning on staying long. David Kelley never intended on making the sublime oddball a regular character. But after seeing all of his compulsive humming, remote-control-toilet-flushing, stomach-gurgling, moment-taking quirks in action, the writer couldn't resist making him a permanent member of the firm.

Ally's life would be a lot duller without Cage, even if stopped pestering her for dates forever. The guy likes to say he's "troubled," and he's right: Cage justifies visits to prostitutes because it's more honest than dating women only to have sex with them . . . that is, if he could get a date. But eccentric as he is, the Little Biscuit's love life is slowly improving. Sexy Renee Radick once expressed interest, and there was more than a little chemistry between Cage and an old law school chum played by Cynthia Stevenson.

Loopy as he is, Cage can't be written off as mere comic relief. Daffy and insecure he may be personally, but professionally Cage is a brilliant, confident lawyer. Outside the office, Ally's dodged his hapless advances, but in the courtroom anyway, he's a mentor. She once even copied his trademark technique of "taking a moment"—that killer silent pause in court that manages to rattle, confuse and mystify others.

Peter MacNicol, the man behind Cage, describes his technique as "a little bit like *The Art of War*" by Lao-Tzu—a canny strategy that more often than not leads to courtroom victory. Those little pauses had an effect on viewers too. In the hyper-chatty world of television, it's not often an actor makes such an impression by keeping his mouth shout.

HE ISN'T RELATED TO TATUM O'NEILL, EITHER

A lot of people assume the Little Biscuit is the big brother of *Little Darlings* star Kristy. Wrong-o. Peter has two sisters who are both lawyers, not 1970s trivia questions. They all grew up in Dallas, Texas, where Peter was born on April 10, 1954. Peter has never appeared on the cover of *Tiger Beat*. However, Kristy's real brother, Jimmy, has.

LET'S KILL ALL THE LAWYERS

After graduating from the University of Minnesota, Peter pursued a successful stage acting career in Manhattan, winning raves at the New York Shakespeare Festival and acting in several Broadway plays. But a precedent was set with his award-winning debut role in Beth Henley's *Crimes of the Heart*—it was the first of times he's played a lawyer.

MacNicol in the movie
Dragonslayer

"*A biscuit is something
warm, doughy, not
sharply defined.
Something rounded,
smooth and inviting.
Actually, I have no
earthly idea. I don't
want to know.*"
—*Peter MacNicol, on the
genesis of his character's
yeasty nickname*

PETER MACNICOL

SHE HAS NO PROBLEM WITH HIS SALIVA FLOW

Since 1986, Peter has been married to Marsue Cumming. They live in L.A. and have two dogs, and no fish.

WHO YA GONNA CALL?

Among his many movie roles—Peter as a sorcerer's apprentice in *Dragonslayer* (back when he looked like Mark Hamill), aspiring writer Stingo in the Meryl Streep bummer *Sophie's Choice*, and a prissy camp counselor in *Addams Family Values*—Peter says the only people who recognize him are kids who loved him as the bizarro Janosz Poha in *Ghostbusters II*.

BREATHE, DAMN YOU!

During the first season of *Chicago Hope*, Peter signed on to play the odd (not Cage-odd, medium-odd) lawyer Alan Birch. A year into the show, Peter wanted out of his contract, hoping to return occasionally as a recurring character. Instead producer David Kelley killed him off.

AND I'M NOT JUST SUCKING UP TO PROVE THERE ARE NO HARD FEELINGS OVER THE *CHICAGO HOPE* THING

After taking the role of John Cage, Peter told *USA Today*, "I don't think anyone since Anton Chekov reaches down so deeply into supporting characters."

Hmm ...don't recall a wattle-fondling scene in *The Cherry Orchard*.

BEAN THERE, DONE THAT

Peter played the straight man to Rowan Atkinson's annoying limey mute in the transatlantic comedy/marketing blitz *Mr. Bean*.

THAT'S NOT SCOTTISH

In addition to geeky pleasures like collecting toy soldiers, old movie posters and old lunch boxes with TV Western themes, like John Cage, Peter gets in touch with his inner William Wallace by playing the bagpipes.

IF PETER MACNICOL HAD A THEME SONG IT WOULD BE

"People Are Strange"

" *He's a moon calf.* "

—MacNicol, on Cage

Phren-Ally-gy

If you could peek inside Ally's head, what would it look like? Well, pink and gooey and—but seriously, even though we already poke around inside that pretty noggin every week, a map of Ally's subconscious would be helpful the next time a spear-chucking infant came around or Ally found herself visiting a trash pile at warp speed. Below, we dabble in phren-Ally-gy (but we're not the first people to think she should have her head examined!):

❶ FANTASY ISLAND

The pain! The pain! Ally deals with it—and other strong feelings—by sending them on a package vacation to this far-out spot. Where she cooks up those vivid visions, parks that Dumpster, and stockpiles the helium that makes Elaine's head swell.

❷ BABYLAND

The Dancing Baby's time-share—where Ally's biological clock anxiety stores spears, in-line skates, and spare diapers.

❸ RAIN DROPS ON ROSES!

Oh, Ally hates it when she's compared to Julie Andrews. Well, it's not true. For one thing, Ally's a hopeless romantic given to sweetie-sweet little homilies about true love, happiness and traditional values, and on her show, she stars in big song and dance numbers ... oh my goodness! That sounds a lot like a certain Austrian governess to us. How do you solve a problem like McBeal-a?

❹ MEOW!

Julie Andrews doesn't live here anymore. Den of Ally the man-eater, whose lusty libido conquered Glenn the artist's model (at least temporarily), slept with family man Jack Dawson, and slammed uptight Ronald Cheanie for not kissing her on the first date. Where the hellion who wants to be treated like a sexual object slips into something a little more comfortable. Watch out boys, she'll chew you up.

❺ INCOMING!

War is hell—especially in Ally's ideological zone, where she can't decide if she wants to bring home the bacon, fry it up in a pan, or call for take-out ...

❻ MY BOY BILL

Billy still is an absentee land-lord in Ally's head, squatting in far more space than he should. Where Ally comes to indulge in destructive nostalgia about the one that got away.

❼ AND JUSTICE FOR ALL ...

There may not always be order in her emotional court, but Ally loves being a lawyer—and she's pretty good at what she does (she's only lost one case, and she turned that baby around on appeal). Mental note: Remember not to hire undocumented worker just in case appointed attorney general.

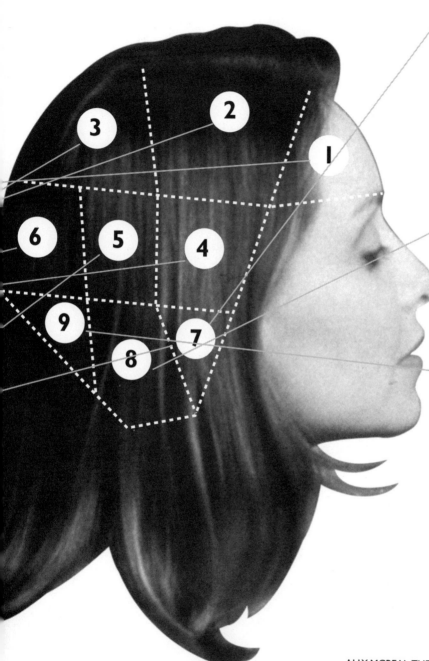

❼ OUCH, I PULLED MY EYELID!

Except for one kickboxing match (and it was emotion, not skill, that guided her body blows then), Ally's not exactly a poster child for Nike. A trick back, aversion to team playing and difficulty walking without falling flat on her bum have kept her off the varsity squad for life . . .

❽ WORK, SUPERMODEL . . .

As they say down at Neiman's, Ally's fashion-forward. The home of her inner personal shopper, who picks out those cutting-edge skirts and killer shoes.

❾ ACK!

Low-rent district, where Ally's inner *Cathy* lives, fretting about state and condition of her all-consuming—and always disap-

McBeal This Look

Like the character who wears them, people either love Ally's garb or hate it. So much ink has been spilled on her hem lines, you'd think it was 1968, not 1998. Working women do wear short skirts pretty regularly these days, and have been wearing them for quite awhile. Not that short—unless they work for MTV—but pretty short.

But like everything else about Ally, her fashion is a never-ending source of conversation and debate. David Kelley has even incorporated the skirt squabble into the show with nasty characters periodically sniping at Ally's courtroom attire. When Ally crossed over to *The Practice*, she got guff from local DA Lara Flynn Boyle about her minis—even though Boyle's skirts aren't exactly knee-cap coverers themselves (and another thing: gaunt Lara Flynn Boyle makes Calista Flockhart look positively corn-fed). Ally's short-short skirts are only a wee bit shorter than the short skirts worn by every other woman in TV land except the leg-impaired Kirstie Alley and Ellen.

So Ally knows that some people think she dresses inappropriately, and she keeps dressing that way anyway. She's a rebel, and we like that she doesn't cross-dress as Janet Reno to be taken seriously. Besides, showing a little gam hardly makes you a traitor to feminism—Gloria Steinem's been wearing Ally-length skirts since 1966.

As for the rest of her look, it's unimpeachably tasteful, and now, extremely popular. Customers have mobbed department stores and boutiques trying to crib the *Ally McBeal* look right down to those adorable Nick & Nora jammies. That's not been lost on the execs at Fox's consumer-products division, who would very much like Ally to follow in the high heels of Jaclyn Smith, Cheryl Tiegs, Kathy Ireland and Kathy Lee and get a signature clothing line (they've also discussed martini accessories, calendars, cards and stationery). But thus far, David Kelley's been cautious with his baby—he doesn't want her rags on the rack at Kmart. Personally, we're holding out for the Ally McBeal lunch box.

But if you want to copy Ally's look, you don't need to kidnap the wardrobe mistress or wear out your VCR freeze frame trying to sketch patterns. All you need is this handy, dandy Ally paper doll—and good credit.

GLOBE PHOTOS

Law Suits: Elements of

Ally-Style

Suits:

What you already know—Ally favors very short skirts (more than 6" above the knee) with long tailored jackets and small sweaters or silk shirts underneath. Putting the Great Hemline Debate aside for just a moment, her suits are modern, but appropriate for most offices (though some of her blouses do get a bit tight and plunge-y).

Shoes:

Ally likes her shoes early '70s retro fused with 1990s cool: lots of strappy sandals with big, chunky heels and mod-looking high-heeled loafers.

Where to Find Them

Until she builds her own third world sweatshop, Ally wears other people's labels—Donna Karan, Tahari, Emporio Armani, Bebe, Parallell, INC. at Macy's, Laundry, and Claudio. We're talking big money here: from $300 and upward per suit. But if you don't want to wait for the polyester Wal-Mart version, you can get good quality, lower-priced versions from Liz Claiborne, Banana Republic, DKNY and Club Monaco. If you want the Ally-length skirts, you may have to get out the sewing machine—at retail, most of the suits stop a little lower on the thigh or even graze the knees. The women's costume designer for *Ally McBeal* shops for her at Saks Fifth Avenue, Bloomingdales, and the boutique Bebe.

Where to Find Them

Ally's shoes are made by Charles David and Kenneth Cole. A good place to track down McBeal-style shoes is Nine West.

EVERETT COLLECTION: © 20TH CENTURY FOX

DOROTHY HANDELMAN

Pajamas

Ally loves her big, soft, comfortable Nick & Nora "counting-sheep" pajamas. So do a lot of other people. Ally's first appearance in her counting sheep-style pair was followed by a massive rush on the stores—and the sleepies sold out pretty much everywhere. Nick & Nora hopes to have more on the shelves by the time you read this.

Where to Find Them

If you are lucky, you may track down the trendy lounge wear at major department stores such as Bloomingdales, for about $65 a pair. But to avoid being disappointed, you can call Nick & Nora in New York at (212) 629-9500 to find out what retailer near you stocks their sleep wear. The Victoria's Secret Catalog also carries the pajamas.

Scarves

Ally digs wearing flowery silk neckerchiefs 1970s-style, but as the season has worn she's stopped wearing them as much as used to. Fashion warning: choose your scarf well, or risk looking like Howdy Doody.

Where to Find Them

Most everywhere, and at wildly varying prices. But for our money the best place for this accessory is the old reliable the Gap.

Hair

Some addled fashion mavens have declared Ally's hair "in," saying she's brought back the "uncomplicated look." Whew, what I relief. We hated it last year when "complicated hair" was so in. Basically folks, Ally has an ever-so-slightly layered and shaped bob—a hairdo that's been around at least since flappers walked the earth. Every so often she puts it up in a loose, messy ponytail. Wow, so can you!

Where to Get This Look

If your hair is limp enough, you can get close to this look for under $30; heck, if you or a friend are semi-accomplished trimmers, you can probably pull it off in your very own bathroom. Most likely Ally is fluffed and gossiped at by some guy with one name and an affected accent. Cost: more than your mortgage.

Furnishings:

Ally's a young professional, and if her clothes are *trop cher*, most of her apartment's furnishings—couches, chairs, lamps and carpets in soft pastel hues—are not. To transform your abode into Allyworld, you need look no further than Pottery Barn and IKEA. But then, if you are a twenty- or thirtysomething female of reasonable means who occasionally watches *Melrose Place*, you already knew that. As the show's core demographic, Ally's creators did their level best to copy *you*.

The Incredible Shrinking TV Lawyer

Read this far and think Ally's a normal-sized woman? Well, then you must hail from Burma. The average American woman is a size 14; Ally splurges on a Ho-Ho and she's a 2 if she's lucky. But she's hardly the first skinny-minnie icon to be foisted on American womanhood, either. Maybe it's the combo that bugs some people so much—that Ally is skinny and occasionally insecure, skinny and occasionally politically incorrect, skinny and needy. Or it could be that on TV, where the camera is supposed to add 10 pounds, looking like you need to gain 10 pounds can be creepy.

But there are naturally little women in the world, too. And if the girl can't help it, why keep beating up on her? She is what she is: skinny. Don't like it? Adjust the horizontal on your set and see if that helps. And one thing must be said for Kelley and Co.: they aren't afraid to poke fun at Ally's weight any more than they are her skirts. On *Melrose Place*, Ally wouldn't be commented on—she'd just be taken as normal. And that's something worth getting angry about. At least Ally lives in a world where large-sized people like *The Practice* lawyer played wonderfully by Camryn Manheim actually exist as more than punch-lines.

> "*I eagerly await the episode, where, in summation, Ally turns to the jury and asks, 'Does this outfit make me look fat?'*"
>
> —*Joyce Millman*, Salon

"I do wish my breasts were bigger. Not huge, but…less small."
—Calista Flockhart, sounding like Ally in Mademoiselle

Mannheim's notable exception aside, though, we have noticed something strange going on among TV lawyers—call it *Thinner* goes to court. Even as our fascination with the law intensifies and legal issues get more muddy, our prime-time attorneys are wasting away to nothingness. Is there an evil government plot, or did nobody notice when Jenny Craig was appointed to the Supreme Court? Whatever the case, the scales of justice are definitely tipping up, up and up:

TV Lawyer:
Perry Mason, chunky-style TV law pioneer
Fighting Weight:
210 pounds with "all you can eat bib" removed
Exercise Regime:
Bench press own weight in flapjacks and Della Street at same time, keep ursine physique toned by winning every case

GLOBE PHOTOS

TV Lawyer:
Rumpole of the Bailey, flabbalicious limey litigator
Fighting Weight:
200 pounds minus wig
Exercise Regime:
Gold medalist, UK Olympic Bangers-and-Mash Chugging Squad

LEAN WAS
ALLY

TV Lawyer:
Stewart Markowitz,
squishy nebbish
from *L.A. Law*
Fighting Weight:
185 pounds with domi-
neering wife detached
Exercise Regime:
Runs 15-minute whine

TV Lawyer:
DA Jack McCoy, Ichabod
Crane-y crime fighter
on *Law & Order*
Fighting Weight:
160 pounds minus
righteous indignation
Exercise Regime:
Keeps lean and mean
throwing the book at
street scum

TV Lawyer:
Ally McBeal,
Beantown Beanpole
Fighting Weight:
Barely breaks 110
with hair wet
Exercise Regime:
Being hurled into
Dumpster is good
for abs

Grrl Friday

Elaine means well, really she does. It's just that she just can't help but poke her little button nose into other people's business. Being a secretary is just her job—and one she's not all great at. Being a gossip is her vocation, and she happens to be very good at it. Ally's got no secrets from her—and that's not for want of trying. Aside from filing legal documents (and baseless sexual harassment law suits), Elaine has many talents. She invented the wrinkle-preventing face bra, and the loneliness-preventing Man CD. She comes to office parties with her very own backup singers. She diminishes Ally's pimples without squeezing them. On a good day, she's been known to use her grapevine powers for good and morph into a Girl Friday with a positive attitude.

Granted, there are those teensy-weensy little flaws. Like Richard, Elaine's compulsively honest, even when it's not the best policy. Her candid testimony on "behalf" of Ally when the State Bar reviewed her boss's emotional stability wasn't exactly helpful. Then there's Elaine's constant breathy vamping and inability not to mash anything in jockey shorts. Elaine proudly calls herself a "slut." Most grating of all is her desperate need to be the center of attention, a need so strong it caused her to sue her friends when she thought Jennifer the mail girl was stealing the spotlight by "flaunting her big alabaster boobies in everybody's faces."

And another thing—she's a big officious, fat-heated know-it-all...who flaunts her big alabaster boobies in everybody's faces. Yet Ally wouldn't dream of firing her.

Firing Elaine would never do; she's far too much fun to have around as all-purpose-office vixen. At bottom her gossip is really good-natured meddling, and the slutty act seems to be just that—an act (men of all shapes and sizes are inexplicably repelled by this cutie). Elaine's not vicious—her only crime is that she likes to pretend she's starring in her own soap opera, *The Young and Litigious*. Which makes her a great part for real-life ex-soap star Jane Krakowski to play.

WHAT EXIT?
Like Calista, 29-year-old Jane grew up in New Jersey. The two had known each other for years: Jane's best friend, Liane Kamena, was Calista's college roomie.

AND THE TONY FOR BEST ROLLER-SKATING GOES TO . . .
Like so many of her *Ally* castmates, Jane considers herself a Broadway baby. But she's the only one who had a big career in musical theater. In addition to singing and skating in Andrew Lloyd Webber's schlocky *Starlight Express*, Jane belted it out in *Once Upon a Mattress*, *Company*, *One Touch of Venus* and *Grand Hotel*, for which she received a Tony nomination.

"Some people love her, some people hate her. Some people love what they hate about her."

—*Jane Krakowski on Elaine-appeal*

JANE KRAKOWSKI

AND THE AWARD FOR THE BEST PERFORMANCE AS AN EVIL TWIN GOES TO ...

While Courtney Thorne-Smith romped in satin sheets on a nighttime soap, Jane is also the only *Ally* cast member to have a long-running role on a daytime drama. She played feisty Rebecca "T.R." Kendall on an NBC series *Search for Tomorrow* from 1984 to 1986, and was nominated for two daytime Emmys. However, like the very-Elaine Susan Lucci, she was passed over by snappish academy members.

HAVE YOU CHECKED THE CHILDREN?

In everybody's favorite date movie, *Fatal Attraction*, Jane had a small role as a baby sitter for severely stressed-out parents Michael Douglas and Anne Archer. Archer was stressed out again in *Clear and Present Danger* with future boss Greg Germann. Jane also appeared in *National Lampoon's Vacation*.

Elaine demonstrates another fascinating invention to her colleagues

SNAPPISH? WELL FIDDLE-DEE-DEE!

Before she was the Miss Scarlett of *Ally McBeal*, Jane wore a hoop skirt in the Halle Berry plantation bodice ripper miniseries *Queen*. Her bonnet and golden ringlets accentuated an already strong resemblance to a limited edition mail-order collectible.

SO THAT'S WHERE ELAINE LEARNED TO BE A SUCH A LOWDOWN HOOCHIE-MAMA!

Jane co-starred in the mistaken identity comedy *Mrs. Winterbourne* with Brendan Frasier and gossipy talk queen Ricki Lake.

SO THAT'S WHERE ELAINE LEARNED . . . THAT LIFE WAS A CABARET?

In 1991, Jane joined a singularly un-sensational chorus line of unhappy house-fraus in the Liza Minnelli tap-dance dramedy *Stepping Out*.

DON'T TELL US BILLY HAS ANOTHER ADMIRER

Jane appears to be stalking Gil Bellows. She appeared with Sarah Jessica Parker in the Broadway hit *Once Upon a Mattress*, after Parker had appeared with Bellows in *Miami Rhapsody* and *The Substance of Fire*. More recently Jane followed his wife Rya Kihlstedt in the independent film *Hudson River Blues*. She also once guest-starred on the Canadian Mountie detective show *Due South*, and creepily enough, Gil happens to be a Canuck. Time to call in the RCMP.

IF JANE HAD A THEME SONG IT WOULD BE . . .

"You're So Jane (You Probably Think This Song Is About You)"

> *"This season has been an amazing ride for all of us."*
>
> —*Jane Krakowski*

Take a letter—and while you're at it, remove the letter opener from my back...

Good help is *so* hard to find—instead of a reliable right arm, Ally has Elaine, who even with the best intentions manages to sabotage her boss. But at least she's never tried to steal her man, steal her job, lace her morning brew with arsenic or frame her for murder. With some prominent sidekicks, *Willingness to Betray* is a resume requisite. At least Elaine's treachery hasn't gotten anybody beheaded by the paper-cutter. And we can't say that for all the errant assistants we know.

ELAINE
Devious Scheme: Puff self up by making boss look nutty
Undermines Boss By: Letting it slip to judge that she's unstable
Rationale for Insubordination: Life's a Snitch

IAGO
Devious Scheme: Eliminate affirmative action for moors in Italian army
Undermines Boss By: Gas-lighting him into believing wife's cheating, setting him up to kill her
Rationale for Insubordination: Venice is murder in the summertime

EVE HARRINGTON
Devious Scheme: Wants to win Tony by sucking up to every Tom, Dick and Harry
Undermines Boss By: Stealing charm school tips, makeup, man, career
Rationale for Insubordination: Likes bumpy rides

THE TEMP
Devious Scheme: Rise up corporate ladder using corpses of colleagues as stairs
Undermines Boss By: Taking credit for work; attempting to hack to pieces
Rationale for Insubordination: Wants to shatter glass ceiling with meat cleaver

National Hair-itage

SAMANTHA STEPHENS
Hairdo: Bewitching blonde
'Do Tell: Not a hair in the world

LAURA PETRIE
Hairdo: Jackie Oh! Hair Dick Van Delicious
'Do Tell: Lacquered locks impervious to pillbox hat dents

THAT GIRL, ANN MARIE
Hairdo: America flipped for gravity-defying flip
'Do Tell: Made New York safe for single girls by having ends that could be used as deadly weapons

MARY RICHARDS
Hairdo: Tressed for Success
'Do Tell: Hair worth throwing hat off for

She's Got...

Samantha Stephens
Leg Story: Charmed peeping neighbors
Hem Length: 60s short

Laura Petrie
Leg Story: Went through more pairs of Capri pants than entire population of Naples
Hem Length: Wore pants in family

That Girl, Ann Marie
Leg Story: Accessorized groovy gams with diamonds and moonbeams
Hem Length: modishly mini

Mary Richards
Leg Story: Legs could take a nothing day, and suddenly make it all seem worthwhile
Hem Length: First mini, then maxi, then midi

FARRAH FAWCETT
Hairdo: Feathered Fantasy
'Do Tell: On wings and a prayer, changed the hair of small town girls forever

MURPHY BROWN
Hairdo: Cokie-Coola
'Do Tell: Loaned hair to sand floors in Lincoln Bedroom

FRIEND-LY RACHEL
Hairdo: Shagnificent
'Do Tell: Luscious layers conquer Jennifer-ation X

ALLY McBEAL
Hairdo: Bob's New-Tart
'Do Tell: Wash-and-wear hair reveals heroine's at split ends

Legs

Charlie's Angel, Jill Monroe
Leg Story: Could run in high heels and shoot straight at same time
Hem Length: Unless under cover in disco or brothel, felt fine in flares

Murphy Brown
Leg Story: Hard-bitten news gal wanted to give leg-up to women in media
Hem Length: Hillary-Happiest Just-Above-the-Knee

Friend-ly Rachel
Leg Story: Legs ran out on wedding day, ran rings around Ross
Hem Length: SoHo Short

Ally McBeal
Leg Story: Thigh-high-Harvardian
Hem Length: Micro-Scopes Trial

It Came From Prime Time

You may be searchin' your CD collection for Vonda's *Ally McBeal* theme song today, but tomorrow it may be just another *Hawaii 5-0* anthem. TV show songs rarely jump from the box to the pop charts, and when they do, the results can be a little embarrassing. Hey, not to dis Vonda, but she's in some pretty motley company. It's hard to know what's worse, unassuming songs that get adopted by television shows and are forever associated with them, or TV-spawned theme songs that cross over into Radioland. Can you believe in 1976, intelligent, discriminating people actually listened to the theme song from *Laverne and Shirley* on the radio—and bought the record? Well, they did—and we have their names right here . . . okay, everybody relax. Your secret is safe for now. Next time you crank up *Songs from Ally McBeal*, mull over how the collection might stack up against these gems:

I Don't Want to Wait—Paula Cole's song was a hit before it made it huge in junior high schools as the theme of WB's teenybopper soap *Dawson's Creek*. But now it's gone from Lilith Fair anthem to a song about getting out of study hall.

Closer to Free—And they call Ally whiny. It seems we'll never be free of those crying, complaining Salinger kids on *Party of Five* who've commandeered this Bo-Deans song for eternity. Charlie didn't have cancer—just a really, really bad migraine.

I'll Be There for You—At the height of *Friends* mania, this relentless Monkees-oid jingle by The Rembrandts was a transatlantic sensation. We don't know what's worse: the song, the memories of the video in which the cast "played" instruments behind the band, or watching the cast twirl balloons and dance in a fountain to it even now. These Rembrandts are no old masters.

The Theme Song from *Greatest American Hero*—Believe it or not, this got on the air back in 1979.

Welcome Back, Kotter—If you remember this theme song, shout ooh-ooh and grab your armpit. Confused an entire nation when lyric "Who'd have thought they'd need ya?" came out "Hooda-bopa-leeja."

Happy Days-Laverne and Shirley **combo**—Back when they were a back-to-back ratings sensation in the mid-1970s, these theme songs were played back-to-back on the radio. Truth be told, the Schotz Brewery anthem is catchy. But the other song is the Potsies . . .

The Rockford Files—Okay, this one rocked. But what was on the B-side? *Barnaby Jones?*

Nadia's Theme—This cheesy instrumental actually came from daytime, not prime time, where it still resides as the music for *The Young and the Restless.* It got its new name when it was used by the sweetheart of 1976, Nadia Comaneci, at the Olympics.

(Warning: if something's a big pop hit in Bucharest, it's probably not that hip.)

Cheers—Wouldn't you like to get away from hearing this song on the radio? When the show premiered, some deejays obviously didn't agree.

C'mon Get Happy—*The Partridge Family* tune was snapped up by David Cassidy-fixated 7-year-old girls in the early 1970s.

Dallas—People in the big D couldn't get enough of their own theme song; some folks (the Dallas Cowgirls) still can't.

Luckily, we're not caught in this Current of Love—It's not for want of trying, but David Hasselhoff's *Baywatch* songs haven't gotten all that much popular air play. Unless you live in Dusseldorf, that is . . .

Ooga-Chaka! Baby Cha-cha Speaks!

Just before this book went to press, Baby Cha-cha, the baby behind Mr. Huggy on *Ally McBeal*, granted an unprecedented first-time ever interview. Although he's reached the heights of fame since his debut on *Ally* in January 5, 1998, Cha-cha has avoided direct contact with media, preferring, as he says, "to let my work speak for itself." But rumors of friction with other cast members and his imminent departure from *Ally McBeal*—culminating with comments by David Kelley that Cha-cha "would not be back" next season, have forced him out of seclusion.

We met with Cha-cha by the pool of his magnificent postmodern home in Pacific Palisades. Wearing Ray-Bans and swaddled in a thick white terry cloth robe, he insisted he bears no ill-will toward anyone at *Ally McBeal*.

TOTALLY UNAUTHORIZED GUIDE TO ALLY MCBEAL: Wow, you look fantastic. Even younger in person.

Cha-cha: Thanks. I've been working out a lot with Cherokee, my personal trainer [tan young woman in spandex aerobics gear enters, bearing tray of wheat germ protein shakes with Terra Chips and pabulum]. Thanks. Cher, give us some privacy, will ya? Love ya, babe.

She's been great with getting off some of the baby fat I had when I first appeared on *Ally McBeal*. The camera really does add 20 pounds.

TUGAM: Cha-Cha, we've all seen the tabloid reports about how you got the part.

Cha-cha: Yeah, well, you know, I just don't know where they get that stuff. Mind if I smoke? [Lights a Marlboro Red]. I never met Michelle Pfeiffer before the show. Okay, once, at an Alan Parker party for *Grease II*, but we were just kids. The truth is, when the show came along, I was minding my own business working in Silicon Valley for a company called Kinetix. I was away from the whole Hollywood scene, but I had a sort of cult following over the Internet. That's how Kelley heard about me.

TUGAM: So how did you become a television star overnight?

Cha-cha: You know, I was talking to Jenna Elfman about this the other day at Sky Bar, and we both were saying how obnoxious it was that people think we just got where we are because we're cute. They see the Land Cruiser and the trips to Mustique, and they say, he's got all this and he's just a baby—who did he sleep with? Well, they didn't see me when I was working 14-hour shifts as a screensaver in Palo Alto, eating Gerber's out of the jar. I paid my dues, did some summer stock, put together a one-man show, and word got out. Kelley told me the show needed oomph. That's what I do: oomph. I'm an oomph person. It was the whole Heather Locklear-*Melrose Place* thing all over again. Let's be honest: I saved them. Don't say thank you, don't invite me to your little parties with

Bochco, that's cool. But you remember, man; you always remember.

TUGAM: Is it true you've become a Scientologist?

Cha-cha: I really don't think my personal value system is anybody's business. But it's true I've done a lot of searching. I feel, at this stage, a real yearning for something, you know? All this success [sweeps hand across landscaped patio and pool], and I feel like such a baby. Cherokee's helped me a lot with the growth thing. I was so two-dimensional before I met her. My life was like a cartoon.

TUGAM: The Viper Room period?

Cha-cha: Yeah, man, I don't even talk to Charlie Sheen anymore [turns away and looks silently out across the Pacific below]. For a baby, I've had to grow up so fast.

TUGAM: You were a big hit when you first appeared on the show—now we're seeing less and less of you. Is it true you were considered by Fox to be another Shannen Doherty?

Cha-cha: I'm not going to comment on Shannen. Shannen and I . . . [looks away again]. The truth is, my appearances on *Ally McBeal* led to other opportunities. I got to do a lot there—throw spears, roller-hockey, and of course dance—and I'm forever grateful to David Kelley for that. The big boys at Fox noticed, and they approached me to do promos for next year's fall shows and other projects next year. Basically,

we've left the door open for next season. I may come back to do a few shows. We're in negotiations. You know, I love David, but we're growing in different directions. It's been a tough few months, but I think we've both learned something here. You know, it's like that line about holding a moonbeam in your hand. I'm a moonbeam, you know? And it's time to go shine my light elsewhere.

TUGAM: There's been a lot of talk of bad blood between you and other cast members.

Cha-cha: That's ridiculous. People just have different expectations of their work relationships, I guess. I mean, you come into a new show with all these unknowns, and you come a *certain level*, like Dyan Cannon with her film career, or me with this whole cult status over the Internet and all, and really, you just can't be everybody's best friend. I've got a life outside the show. I will say there was a certain resentment of the exposure I was getting.

TUGAM: Is it true Calista demanded to have you fired?

Cha-cha: [Lights another cigarette.] Some things are too painful to revisit right now. You know, the star is the star, and sometimes they get to thinking there's room for only one. But you know, the people you pass on the way up, you pass on your way back down. I saw Baby Huey go into rehab for the third time the other day. Jesus.

TUGAM: I'm sorry. On a lighter note, what did you think of the show's music?

Cha-cha: Well, I'm a dancer first and foremost, as you know. So anything that I can get jiggy with, well, I love. Personally, I'm not really into those oldies. I'm more of techno-house kind of a guy. I used to go to a lot of raves out in the Valley back in the day. [Dons black "X-Files" hat.] Duchovny sent me this down from Vancouver. Gotta watch the skin, you know. Baby.

TUGAM: Cha-cha, thanks so much for setting the record straight.

Cha-cha: Hey no sweat, man. [Gives soul brother handshake and quick hug.] Watch for coyotes on your way back into town. Cherokee, can you show them out? Thanks, babe.

DOUBLE YOUR PLEASURE!

They're goofy, groovy, and always on hand to dance with Ally or Renee—they're the cult sensation known as the Dancing Twins! Here are a few far-out tidbits about them:

- Before becoming the Dancing Twins, they were "The Flying Cohen Brothers."

- On TV, they have goofed-off on *Seinfeld*, *Mad About You* and *Baywatch*.

- Steve Cohen served as a double for Jim Carrey in *Batman Forever* and *The Cable Guy*. Both claim Carrey as their biggest role model.

- They choreograph all their own dance moves, which include "Robocop," the "Funky Chicken" and "The Train."

- They like to do karate kicks while dancing, although it's not a tribute to Renee Radick's martial arts abilities. It's a tribute to Elvis Presley's classic Vegas stage-show maneuver in his white jumpsuit period.

- Among the other talents they claim: unicycling, ping-pong, accordion playing, plate-spinning, making balloon animals, typing 101 words per minute, solving tough crosswords and, er, body-building.

- They are single-handedly trying to bring back the white-shoes-and-matching-belt look. Good luck.

DYAN CANNON

To Dy For!

Jennifer "Whipper Cone" was a whole lotta woman for a stripling like Richard Fish to try and hold on to. But when she dumped the wattle-fiddler after catching him with Janet Reno for the second time, it was time to pray she'd come back for thirds. No wonder his heart was broken—this fiftysomething gal is as alluring and buffed as a school girl and possessed of a sexual appetite of Catherine the Great-style proportions. But in her courtroom, the Whip's as no-nonsense as Judge Judy (plus nuked blond hair and a perma-tan). Whipper is a woman of substance and very strong opinions, but she's smart enough and big enough to admit when she's wrong. After initially reporting Ally to the Bar Association for being nutty, Whipper came to realize she'd been subjecting Ally to a sexist double standard, and went on to bail our heroine out of a jam.

Besides great legs, the two women share the fact that they're romantics at heart—though Whipper isn't given to slap-sticky daydreams. But like Ally, the twice-divorced Whipper's an independent woman who yearns for a steady man. Toward the end of the season, it looked like she was ready to give Fish one more chance. However it turns out, let's hope David Kelley keeps her chambers at the Suffolk County Courthouse permanently. Kelley has said that Cannon is the living, breathing embodiment of the Whip—she's tough, and still reeks of show-biz slut glamour even in her AARP years. If her role often lurches into self-parody, Cannon gets the joke. Here's a woman who's obviously been stretched, pulled and collagen-ed six ways from Sunday who has to regularly call attention to her wattle, for pity's sake. And doesn't seem to mind a bit.

"My boyfriend checks out my wattle now."
—*Dyan Cannon*

IT'S GREEK FOR MOST BEAUTIFUL-SCHMOOTIFUL; I WAS THE ONE MARRIED TO CARY GRANT

Dyan was born Samile Diane Friesen in 1938 in Tacoma, Washington. Because Samile Friesen is no kind of a name for anybody, let alone a glamorous starlet, Dyan got a more Hollywood moniker, later adopting the quirky spelling, which ain't half as quirky as Diahann Carrol's.

OTHER FAMOUS CANNONS

Big Bertha; the Guns of Navarone; hefty detective played by hefty actor William Conrad in 1970s.

WE PREFER THE TERM "VIRTUE-IMPAIRED"

Halliwell's Film Guide describes Dyan as an American leading actress who tends to play floozies. Dyan's first role was as a gangster's moll in the 1959 flick *The Rise and Fall of Legs Diamond*, and it's been one long trip downtown in the paddywagon ever since.

TO CATCH A CARY

Dyan's work in film and television in the early 1960s didn't garner her much attention, but her 1965 marriage to perma-stud Cary Grant made her a household name. The pair divorced in 1968, just as Dyan's career began to take off. They have a daughter, Jennifer, who appeared as Steve Sanders's girlfriend on *Beverly Hills 90210*.

SETH POPPEL YEARBOOK ARCHIVES

TURN ON, TUNE IN, MAKE OUT:

Dyan became a major movie star after starring in the now-quaint free-love comedy *Bob and Carol and Ted and Alice* with Robert Culp, Natalie Wood and Elliot Gould. She also starred in the paisley sex romps *Doctors' Wives* and *The Love Machine*, won raves for her performances as a cuckolded wife in *Such Good Friends* (perhaps because she had to pretend to love wattle-ly James Coco), and appeared in the cult thriller *The Last of Sheila*, which co-stars fellow pinup Raquel Welch.

EVERY MAN IN AMERICA WANTED TO BUY HER A TAB

Exhaustive studies confirm that Dyan Cannon was undoubtedly the Grooviest Chick in the World between 1969 and 1975.

AND SOMEHOW, THEY OVERLOOKED HER PERFORMANCE IN REVENGE OF THE PINK PANTHER

Dyan was nominated for best supporting actress for her work in *Heaven Can Wait* with Warren Beatty, another pretty face who made a career out of playing floozies. Maggie Smith, a not-so-pretty face who made a career of playing anti-floozies, copped the statue for playing an academy award nominee in the *Love Boat*-like *Plaza Suite*.

AWFUL! AWFUL!

Although Dyan starred with Christopher Reeve in *Deathtrap* and Gil Bellows's employer Al Pacino in *Author! Author!*, by the 1980s her movie pickings were slim. Selected slim pickings: *Caddy Shack II*, *Eight Heads in a Duffle Bag*.

GIMME A "C"! (III)

While she's never been a cheerleader-type, Dyan is a long-time fixture at Los Angeles Lakers' games—cheering for and arguing with players courtside.

IF DYAN CANNON HAD A THEME SONG, IT WOULD BE ...

"I Will Survive"

GLOBE PHOTOS

According to her chart, she's a clear-headed type who respects tradition and the law but relishes a good argument.

She's also got an authoritarian streak that allows her to be strictly fair, even if that hurts loved ones.

Dyan Cannon
Born: January 4, 1937
Tacoma, Washington
Star: Capricorn

It might also explain why dating a wattle-fondler doesn't give the Whip more pause. But Dyan's no starchy conservative (one look at those locks will tell you that)—she's a progressive who never simply accepts the status quo.

Judging by the stars, Capricorn Dyan would make as good a jurist as Judge Whipper.

Decades of lusty celluloid cavorting is explained by astrological inclinations to sexual experimentation and mistrust of traditional marriage (somebody should have warned Cary Grant).

GLOBE PHOTOS

CALISTA'S CONSTELLATION

Who Says She's Not the Center of the Universe?

Calista Flockhart hasn't made that many films, and yet she's already forever linked to just about every major star in Hollywood. How, you ask? Well, she starred as supermarket checkout clerk in the bleak *Telling Lies in America* with none other than the infamous Kevin Bacon. But Calista is the nexus of her very own web of celebrities. Explore the connections below, and you'll see that even if Bridget Fonda had gotten the role of Ally McBeal, Calista would be less than six steps away from her castmates on the show—and not a few of *Ally*'s guest stars! When you play Six Degrees of Calista Flockhart, the possibilities are endless. Below are a few ways to link Allywood with the rest of Hollywood. Can you think of some more?

Calista Flockhart
appeared in New York in a live reading of "The Vagina Monologues" with **Winona Ryder**, who was in *Lucas* with **Courtney Thorne-Smith**, who was on *Melrose Place* with **Andrew Shue**, who was in *The Rainmaker* with **Claire Danes**, whose best friend on *My So-Called Life* was *Ally* guest star ... **Wilson Cruz!**

Courtney Thorne-Smith
starred with **Lisa Rinna** on *Melrose Place*, whose husband, **Harry Hamlin**, in *Making Love* was the gay husband of *Ally* guest star . . .
Kate Jackson

Calista Flockhart
appeared in New York in "The Vagina Monologues," written by **Eve Ensler**, stepmother of **Dylan McDermott**, who appeared in *Home for the Holidays*, directed by **Jodie Foster**, who starred with **Robert DeNiro** in *Taxi Driver*, who also starred in *The King of Comedy* with *Ally* guest lawyer . . .
Sandra Bernhard

Calista Flockhart's
father in *The Birdcage* was played by **Gene Hackman**, who was in *Narrow Margin* with **Anne Archer**, who was in *Clear and Present Danger* with **Greg Germann** AND *Fatal Attraction* with **Jane Krakowski**, who was in *Hudson River Blues* with **Rya Khilstedt**, who is married to . . .
Gil Bellows

Meanwhile, Calista's
mother in *The Birdcage* was **Dianne Wiest**, who starred in *Hannah and Her Sisters* with **Mia Farrow**, who was spooked in *Rosemary's Baby* by . . . Judge Happy Boyle himself . . .
Phil Leeds!

Mia Farrow
was also in *Crimes and Misdemeanors* with **Alan Alda**, who starred in *The Four Seasons* with *Ally* guest **Brenda Vaccaro** and *1600 Pennsylvania Avenue* with *Ally* guest . . . **Tate Donovan**

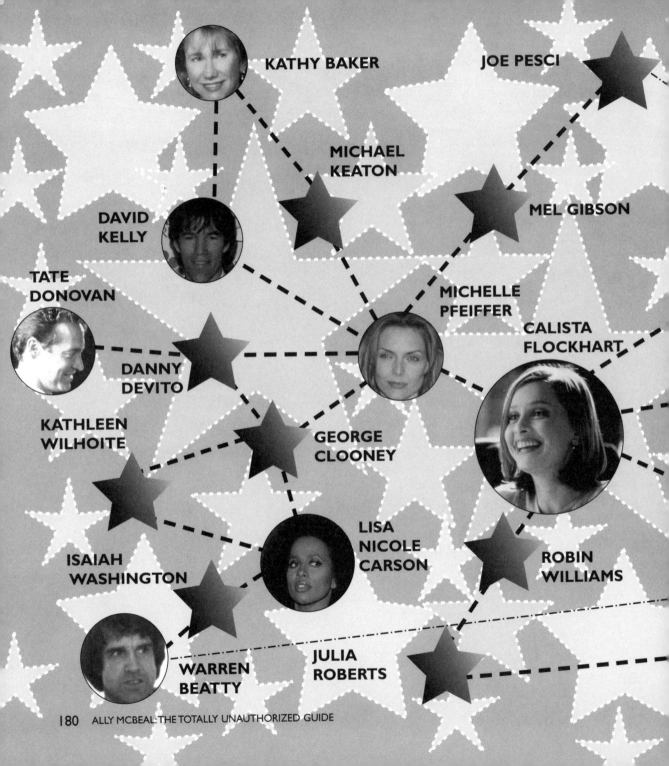

KATHY BAKER

JOE PESCI

MICHAEL KEATON

MEL GIBSON

DAVID KELLY

TATE DONOVAN

MICHELLE PFEIFFER

CALISTA FLOCKHART

DANNY DEVITO

KATHLEEN WILHOITE

GEORGE CLOONEY

ISAIAH WASHINGTON

LISA NICOLE CARSON

ROBIN WILLIAMS

WARREN BEATTY

JULIA ROBERTS

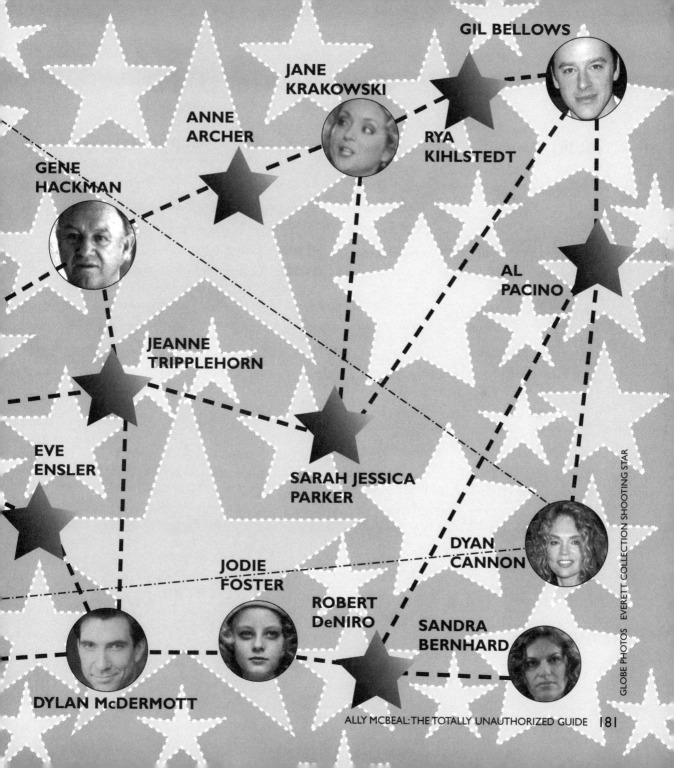

GIL BELLOWS

JANE
KRAKOWSKI

ANNE
ARCHER

RYA
KIHLSTEDT

GENE
HACKMAN

AL
PACINO

JEANNE
TRIPPLEHORN

EVE
ENSLER

SARAH JESSICA
PARKER

DYAN
CANNON

JODIE
FOSTER

ROBERT
DeNIRO

SANDRA
BERNHARD

DYLAN McDERMOTT

Calista Flockhart
will star in *A Midsummer Night's Dream* with **Kevin Kline,** who was in *Sophie's Choice* with **Peter MacNicol,** who is in the upcoming movie *Baby Geniuses* with the . . .
Dancing Twins!

Peter MacNicol
was also in *Sophie's Choice* with **Meryl Streep,** who was in *Plenty* with *Ally* shrink **Tracey Ullman** and *The River Wild* with **Kevin Bacon,** who was in *Telling Lies in America* with . . .
Calista Flockhart

Calista Flockhart
was in the Broadway production of *The Three Sisters* with **Jeanne Tripplehorn,** who was in *'Til There Was You* with **Dylan McDermott** and **Sarah Jessica Parker,** who was in *Miami Rhapsody* with **Gil Bellows,** who was in *Looking for Richard* with **Al Pacino,** who was in *Author! Author!* with . . .
Dyan Cannon

Also, **Calista Flockhart** was in the Broadway production of *The Three Sisters* with **Jeanne Tripplehorn,** who was in *'Til There Was You* with **Sarah Jessica Parker** who was In *Once Upon a Mattress* with . . .
Jane Krakowski

Calista Flockhart was in *The Birdcage* with **Robin Williams,** who was in *Hook* with **Julia Roberts,** who broke off an engagement with . . .
Dylan McDermott

Calista Flockhart
was in *A Midsummer Night's Dream* with **Michelle Pfeiffer**, who was in
One Fine Day with **George Clooney**, who appeared on *ER* with **Lisa
Nicole Carson** and *Ally* guest . . .
Kathleen Wilhoite

Lisa Nicole Carson
was in *Love Jones* with *Ally* guest and Renee kickboxing victim **Isaiah
Washington**, who was in *Bulworth* with **Warren Beatty**, who starred in
Heaven Can Wait with . . .
Dyan Cannon

Calista Flockhart
appears with **David Kelley**'s wife **Michelle Pfeiffer** in *A Midsummer
Night's Dream*, who was in *Tequila Sunrise* with **Mel Gibson,** who was in
Lethal Weapon with **Joe Pesci**, who was in *Eight Heads in a Dufflebag* with . . .
Dyan Cannon

Michelle Pfeiffer
was in *Batman Returns* with **Danny DeVito**, who was the Hercules' side-
kick in the Disney film starring the voice of *Ally* guest . . .
Tate Donovan

Calista Flockhart
was in *A Midsummer Night's Dream* with **Michelle Pfeiffer**, who was in
Batman Returns with **Michael Keaton**, who was in *Clean and Sober* with
Ally guest star **Kathy Baker**, who starred in *Picket Fences*, which was pro-
duced by . . .
David Kelley

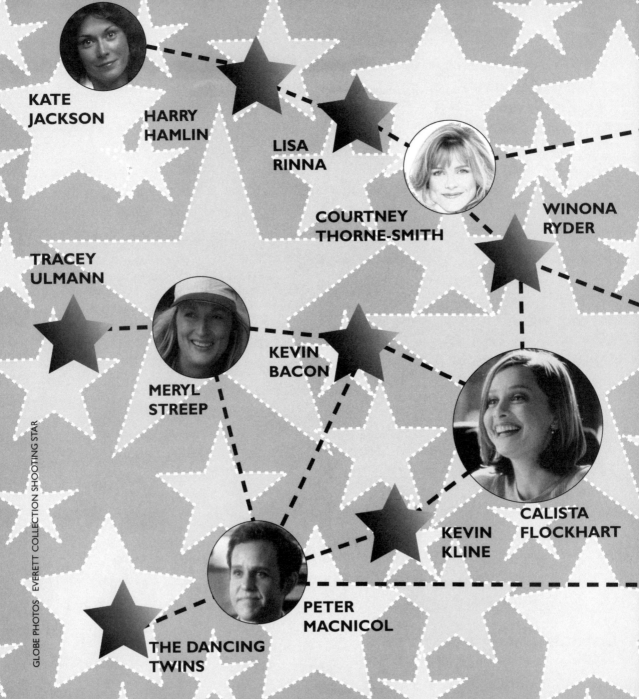

KATE
JACKSON

HARRY
HAMLIN

LISA
RINNA

COURTNEY
THORNE-SMITH

WINONA
RYDER

TRACEY
ULMANN

MERYL
STREEP

KEVIN
BACON

CALISTA
FLOCKHART

KEVIN
KLINE

PETER
MACNICOL

THE DANCING
TWINS

GLOBE PHOTOS   EVERETT COLLECTION   SHOOTING STAR

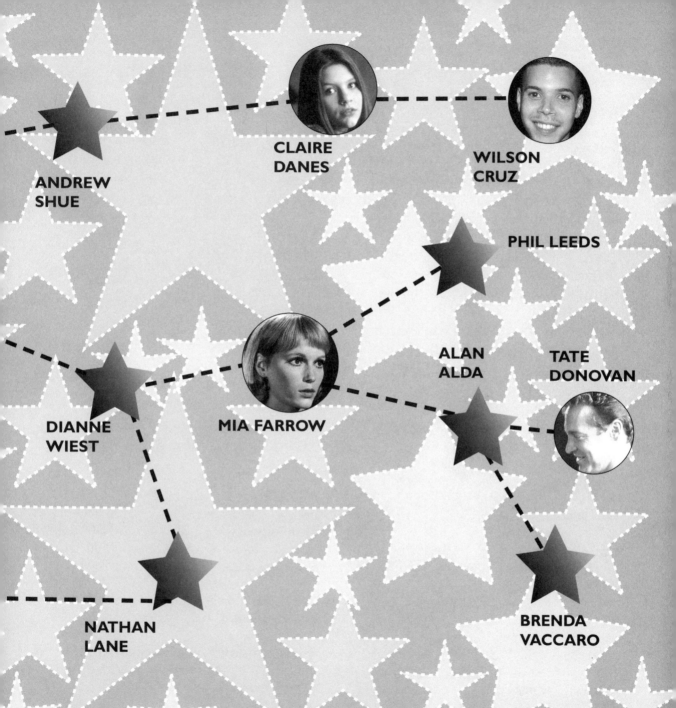

CLAIRE
DANES

WILSON
CRUZ

ANDREW
SHUE

PHIL LEEDS

ALAN
ALDA

TATE
DONOVAN

DIANNE
WIEST

MIA FARROW

NATHAN
LANE

BRENDA
VACCARO

Ally Online

You don't have to move to Boston to meet Ally McBeal—she's the queen of cyberspace. In the year since the show's debut literally hundreds—perhaps thousands—of web sites devoted to Ally have sprung up—the Dancing Twins even have their own electronic homepage.

Finding Ally online can be easy as typing in her name—the number of excellent, comprehensive sites featuring episodes, character sketches and discussion groups is a testament to both Ally's appeal and the intelligence and devotion of her fans.

This is far from a complete listing of Ally-related areas on the Net (to list them all would take another book), but it will definitely get you searchin' with your browser tonight.

DISCLAIMER: SITES COME AND GO, SO ADDRESSES MAY CHANGE

"Ally McBeal makes me laugh, cry and think about life and love. It's that simple."
—Dana Hagerty, mistress of Ally McBeal's most fan-atical web site

---

The Official Ally McBeal Website
www.foxworld.com
This is officially a good place to delve into Ally-lore. It has a comprehensive episode list and cast information, plus cool bouncing graphics and tons of pix.

Dana Hagerty's Ally McBeal Page
www.geocities.com/Hollwood/Hills/2927/
This is a bonanza—an electronic octopus with tentacles reaching out to seemingly every Ally site there is. For anyone's money, it's definitely the best place to go for any Ally related news or gossip. Hagerty also has her own info-packed Ally newsletter delivered daily to your in-box—visit the web site or email her at missday@yahoo.com to get on board.

Ally McBeal [Richard Thal]
http://members.home.com/amcb/
Another huge Ally site, but especially worthwhile for its Ally McBeal Stress Reduction Kit. There is also a fan fiction mailing list.

Chris Kelley's Dancin' Romancin' Heart Stealin' Ally McBeal Worship Page
miavx1.muohio.edu/~woolarjc/ally.html
This is an Ally page with 'tude. Worthwhile for sass quotient alone.

The Ally McBeal Archive
wonko.inow.com/wilco/entertain-
ment/allymcbeal/index.html
Just what it says—loads of background information on your show of shows.

Love, Ally McBeal
members.aol.com/flyngmonke/
index.html
If you are hooked on Ally's sound track but
can't remember the name of a song, this is
the place to go. It lists music titles and
artists for every song in every episode.

Ally McBeal's Little Black Book
www.amherst.edu/~lebaer/amcbeal
Another big links page to Ally and Ally-related sites all around the net.

Sports Fans Guide to Ally McBeal
www.geocities.com/Hollywood/
Hills/3384/Ally-1.htm
Okay, tough guy, admit that when you are
watching Monday Night Football, you really
want to know if Richard got back with the
Whipper. Now you can do both . . .

Just Calista Flockhart
www.geocities.com/Hollywood/
Boulevard/9865
Just one of seemingly thousands of web
pages for Calista, and a very good one at
that. **CelebSite**, a big archive of celebrity
bios, also has a good one.

Sometimes There's Only One Fish
www.geocities.com/TelevisionCity/
set/7950/
Feeling starved for Fish food? This is one
great big bowl full of Fishisms and all manner
of Fish lore.

Courtney Thorne-Smith
www.courtneythornesmith.com/index.
html
Georgia sympathizers, you've found a home.
Both of you.

The Peter MacNicol Home Page
www.west.net/~phantm/
Troubled by your ignorance of Peter
MacNicol's career? Take a moment to find
out more about him.

The Music of Vonda Shepard
http://www.vesperally.com/
www.vesperalley.com/shepard.htm
This is the official Vonda Shepard site,
but there are others as well.

Official Dancing Twins Website
members.aol.com/allytwins/
The far-out Cohen twins boogie in animated
pictures on this site.

The Unofficial Dancing Baby Home
baby.nwlink.com/
Baby Cha-cha Central for those who love to
watch that baby dance . . .

Help Me, Vonda!

How you react to Vonda Shepard often directly correlates to your opinion of *Ally McBeal*. Fans think her husky ballads sum up the mood of the show—and female singlehood—perfectly. They can't get enough of her. Which is a good thing, because Vonda Shepard sings a lot in every single episode, crooning numbers like "Tell Him" if Ally's in a good mood, or "Walk Away Renee" if she's feeling blue. She also provides background noise for most of the bar scenes, and of course, she wrote the theme song. Basically, we're talking full-on *Vondapalooza* once a week.

So it's not surprising that people who aren't so hot on *Ally McBeal* often don't find "The Singer," as she's billed on the show, so Vonda-ful. Just as some critics find *Ally* a big gooey lump of cheap, manipulative sentiment, they also find Vonda's music as phony-baloney as a Hallmark card. Oh, and some just don't like her voice. But even some fans wonder if Vonda can really go on singing every single song in the entire show so *gawl-dang* slowly. Sometimes it sounds as if she's held open the once-boppy "Hooked on a Feelin' " and forced it to guzzle bad gin and 'ludes.

Of course hordes of people flat-out adore Vonda, even some who wish Ally would just put a sock in it. Her 1998 album, *Songs from Ally McBeal Featuring Vonda Shepard*, has taken off like a rocket, prompting a 40-city concert tour. For a 34-year-old trouper who had been playing around the southern California club scene for more than a decade when the *Ally McBeal* gig came around, it's a sweet reward.

What's next for Vonda? Perhaps she'll get to actually talk to Ally in an episode, even get to walk out of that bar she's permanently trapped in. Maybe David Kelley, who picks all the show's music and frequently teases her about her preference for a lazy tempo, will actually get Vonda to *a tempo*. What we know for sure: in an era when pretty women with guitars are a dime a dozen, Vonda Shepard is lucky enough to give command performances once a week to a crowd of 15 million fans.

> "I feel certain similarities to Ally, just being a career woman, going home at night and facing your life."
>
> —*Vonda Shepard, in* People

VONDA SHEPARD

IT'S GREEK FOR "COULDN'T CHOOSE BETWEEN WANDA AND VERLEEN WHEN I WENT INTO LABOR IN THE BACK OF A PICKUP TRUCK"

Vonda Shepard may have a countrified name, but she grew up in cosmopolitan Los Angeles, the daughter of an actor and a fashion model with an equally unique name, Hadria. Vonda's mother walked out of the family when she was 10, leaving her father to raise four daughters alone.

OKAY, BUT YOU BETTER HAVE A SIGNED PERMISSION SLIP TO HANG OUT IN JAMES TAYLOR'S HOT TUB

From the age of 7, Vonda was playing the piano 8 hours a day. Her love of music was so great that at 16, she begged her father to allow her to drop out of high school and pursue a music career full-time. In 1984, at the age of 20, she landed a plumb job as a back-up singer and keyboardist.

NOT EVEN A ONE-HIT VONDA

Although she'd developed a small following of L.A. fans, Vonda's 1989 debut record, Vonda Shepard, sold poorly. After a 1992 album, The Radical Light, failed to chart, she was dropped by Reprise Records.

IF VONDA SHEPARD HAD A THEME SONG, IT WOULD BE:

"I Only Vonda Be With You"

THE SONG "LAWYERS IN LOVE" WAS A GOOD OMEN ...

After being dropped by her label, Vonda took a job as a backup singer for Jackson Brown and contemplated quitting the music business. Meditation helped her out of her depression, and she released another album, It's Good for Eve, in 1996. Around the same time, she was approached by David Kelley to sing on his show after a Hollywood club date.

... BUT IT'S STILL A TERRIBLE SONG

Another terrible song is "Tracy," by the Cuff Links, which happens to be the official theme song of Ally's therapist Tracey Clark. It was the first pop song on Ally to be heard performed by the original artists, not as covered by Vonda.

I'VE LOOKED AT GUYS FROM BOTH SIDES NOW

Vonda's long-time collaborator and ex-boyfriend is guitarist Michael Landau, who has played on many of Joni Mitchell's albums.

MICHELLE, YOU'RE SWELL.

Kelley was a longtime fan who'd been introduced to Vonda's music by his wife Michelle Pfeiffer, who first caught her act back in 1980. When Vonda saw how she looked on the first episode of Ally McBeal, she was horrified by her appearance—but soul sister Michelle helped out with makeover tips.

Like any television series, Ally McBeal *will have to end. And the happiest ending I could wish is that its romance with the audience stay interesting and unpredictable.*

—*Margo Jefferson*, The New York Times